Oregon Backroads Guide
To the Pacific Crest Trail

Volume One

A Twisting Journey

Ed W. McBee

Two Hats Publishing, LLC
Jacksonville, Oregon

Looking north from Howard Prairie, Mt. McLoughlin, elevation 9,495 feet, stands in the distance.

© 2014 Ed W. McBee
Two Hats Publishing, LLC
Jacksonville, Oregon
Printed by Gorham Printing, Centralia, Washington
Order this book on-line at: OregonBackroads.com
ISBN: 978-0-9904340-0-9   First Edition

All Rights Reserved. No part of this publication, except for brief quotes in printed reviews, may be reproduced, stored in a retrieval system, or transmitted in any form or by any means, electronic, mechanical, photocopying, recording, or otherwise without prior written permission from the author. All photos and text by author except where noted.

Book Design, Cover & Typography: Linda Pinkham
Editors: Linda F. Kestner, Linda Pinkham
Maps: Ed W. McBee

The author and publishers are not responsible for injuries or accidents sustained by readers who follow activities described in this book. All maps and descriptions contained within this guide are subject to change and should be used alongside maps issued by the Forest Service referenced in the Guide.

*Two roads diverged in a wood and I —
I took the one less traveled by,
and that has made all the difference.*

—Robert Frost

ACKNOWLEDGMENTS

Writing and researching Volume One of the *Backroads Guide* has given me the chance to interact with many people I wouldn't ordinarily meet in my work-a-day world. Certainly this book is a work of many of those I've met along the way. Originally, I was inspired to pursue this work by the existence of the Pacific Crest Trail and the many hikers who've accepted its challenges but like most journeys, many paths have opened up.

Long distance hikers along the PCT ship supplies ahead to points along the way north. The logistics of hiking a more then 2,000 mile trail can be daunting and even the best laid plans sometimes go south. Missed connections, pilfered caches, hell, or even high water can all affect traveler's plans.

In keeping with the spirit of the traveler who wants to learn what lies ahead, the unknown is part of the equation. Unknown to the hiker are those people they can expect to meet along the way (fellow hikers and "civilians") who supply information, food, shelter, a hand through a rough spot, or even a band-aid for a blister…"Trail Angels" are what the hikers call them, and without them success is almost impossible.

Writing a book can be like long distance hiking with many challenges ahead for the writer, and just like the hiker, the unknown is part of the equation. I would like to say thank you to the many people who contributed advice, encouragement, and a helping hand through the rough spots, you've been like "Book Angels" to me, showing up when I needed a nudge in the right direction.

Linda Pinkham	Frank Kukla
Diane Wallace	Linda Kestner
Mom & Dad	Dennis Kruse
Byron Marron	Constance & David Jesser

And all of my many friends who explored the high country with me over the years — Rick Curtis, Tom Barnett, Carol Swanton, Joel Manjarris, and many others.

CONTENTS

ACKNOWLEDGMENTS iv
MAP LIST vi
    Introduction: A Twisting Journey 1
    Taking the Scenic Route 3
    Why This Guide Is Useful 9
    About the Author 18
REGION ONE: Jacksonville to Emigrant Lake 19
    Route Description 21
    Road Notes 24
REGION TWO: Ashland to Fort Klamath 59
    Route Description 61
    Road Notes 65
REGION THREE: Fort Klamath to Lemolo Lake 101
    Route Description 103
    Road Notes 106
REGION FOUR: Lemolo Lake to Odell Lake 141
    Route Description 143
    Road Notes 146
INDEX 179

MAPS

REGION ONE: Jacksonville to Emigrant Lake
Map R1.1: Main Route 23
Map R1.2: Jacksonville to Silver Fork Gap 24
Map R1.3: Silver Fork Gap Options 35
Map R1.4: Wrangle Gap to Mt. Ashland 46
Map R1.5: Mt. Ashland to Highway 66 54

REGION TWO: Ashland to Fort Klamath
Map R2.1: Main Route 64
Map R2.2: Emigrant Lake to Hyatt Lake 69
Map R2.3: Hyatt Lake to Pederson Sno-Park 79
Map R2.4: Lake of the Woods to Fort Klamath 84

REGION THREE: Fort Klamath to Lemolo Lake
Map R3.1: Main Route 105
Map R3.2: Crater Lake 111
Map R3.3: Diamond Lake Area 127
Map R3.4: Lemolo Lake Area 134

REGION FOUR: Lemolo Lake to Odell Lake
Map R4.1: Main Route 145
Map R4.2: Lemolo Lake Area 147
Map R4.3: Heading North from Lemolo Lake 156
Map R4.4: Optional Windigo Pass Route 158
Map R4.5: Timpanogas Lake to Willamette Pass...........163

OREGON BACKROADS GUIDE TO THE PACIFIC CREST TRAIL
A Twisting Journey

A Journey Calls...
Exploring places, learning our histories, and meeting others
Along the way are rewards enough for taking any journey.
Secrets learned of this beautiful and interesting
World around us heightens our experience.
Feeling a connection to those who've walked this land for
Thousands of years before us and the
Forces that sculpted these mountains of fire and ice,
We begin to find our place in this timeless land.
Perhaps with eyes more fully open
We can better love this place called **Oregon**.
My friend, there are places and things we've not seen before
And good times to be had.
Shall we see what lies ahead?

"The initial Mystery that attends any journey is: How did the traveler reach his starting point in the first place?"

— *Louise Bogan, American Poet Laureate*

Oregon Backroads Guide to the Pacific Crest Trail

So there we were, rear wheel balanced on the edge of a serious precipice. On the CD player Bob Marley sang "Don't worry…'bout a thing…cause every little thing…is gonna be alright." Bob's prophetic words were eventually proven true but I wasn't so sure at that moment. My own fault I guess for trusting a Forest Service "visitors" map. A half-hour before this we were at a five-way intersection, high in the mountains of Oregon.

My (not inexpensive) map showed this as a three-way intersection. Discovering the signs marking any of these various road options were either missing or SUBAR (Shot Up Beyond All Recognition), I stopped. Consulting the runes and the aforementioned map, I took the road that seemed to lead in the right direction.

Trouble reared its ugly head when the tree branches reached their fingers closer to the paintwork. Weeds started to appear between the wheel tracks. I instinctively started to look for a place to turn this circus around, but no such luck. The road ended abruptly at a washout…

Brio the Cowdog has become an expert backseat driver, always alert for danger (and squirrels).

Introduction: A Twisting Journey

Dang…It was time to see if I was born with the back-up gene or not. Employing my innate, manly ability to fool myself, I turned up the music and shifted 'er into "R." Carefully… we edged down the mountain backwards.

'Brio' the cowdog, monitoring our course by hanging his head out the passenger window, woofed his concern as the road began to crumble away.

Heeding his warning, I incrementally turned the steering wheel and so adjusted our trajectory as to safely deliver us to a turnaround. Whew… another close one.

My goal was to drive the backroads of Oregon from California to Washington, avoiding the clutter of Interstate 5. Sounds easy enough, right?

Shadowing the **PCT (Pacific Crest Trail)**, I wanted to learn more about this amazing state of Oregon I now call home. Exploring a **backroad version of the Pacific Crest Trail** was the plan, wandering around a maze of unmarked logging roads wasn't what I had in mind.

"Must be a better way than this," I muttered to the cowdog… And so this guide began.

TAKING THE SCENIC ROUTE

OK. Let's back this story up a lot of years. My family traveled extensively in the United States as I was growing up in Kansas, and I eventually traveled to all 50 states. I have fond memories of fighting with my big sister in the backseat of the family station wagon as we traveled across North America.

Dad was a map guy and always wanted to take the "scenic route" along the backroads. Mom was willing as long as we didn't encounter any mountains…and when we did, Mom would often threaten to get out of the car and walk the rest of the way. Fortunately, Dad never gave in to the temptation to leave her in the Rockies, and we all moved forward together in the end.

Growing up in Kansas I belonged to the Boy Scouts, Troop 606 in Wichita (go Roadrunner Patrol!). Our troop was very active and we did some kind of monthly outdoor activity come rain, shine, or January.

I had the opportunity to backpack and camp in the Rocky Mountains of Colorado and New Mexico with the Scouts. Certainly a great experience for 13- to 14-year-old kids; the skills of outdoor living learned at that tender age are something I still use.

I was impressed with the stunning beauty of the mountain landscapes. Trout streams meandering through high country meadows beckoned us onward to explore the surrounding canyons and peaks. At night, camping under the cloak of a moonless sky, the Milky Way arching above us seemed impossibly bright.

If magic exists in this world it can surely be found in these rocky, wild places. For a kid from Kansas it seemed like an endless playground. Today when I find myself in the mountains, I feel that Zen of sun-washed high country and big skies, a place of many possibilities.

WASHINGTON IS NOTHING LIKE KANSAS

When I was 14 my parents moved the family from Kansas to the town of Mukilteo in Washington State. Dad was employed by Boeing and was involved with the production and roll-out of the first 747 jetliner.

Transported from the flat lands of Kansas to Puget Sound, we were suddenly surrounded by big trees, snow-capped volcanoes, and the tang of saltwater. That winter, my older sister (Deb) and I learned how to snow ski at Stevens Pass, in the Cascades east of Everett, Washington.

We weren't in Kansas anymore that was for sure…

After arriving in Washington, I joined a Scout troop based in Everett. One of the volunteer projects we were involved with was working on a section of existing trail near Stevens Pass that would eventually become part of the Pacific Crest Trail

Introduction: A Twisting Journey

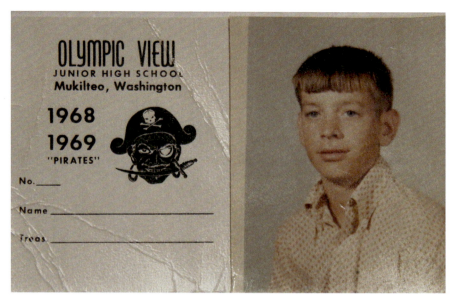

The Boy with Bangs — the author trying to look cool at the age of 14.

(PCT). We spent a beautiful fall day in the High Cascades armed with pulaskis, shovels, and crowbars carving an improvement on this small section of trail.

In Washington, California, and Oregon, the PCT is largely cobbled together from existing routes pioneered by mountaineering groups in all three states starting in the 1920s and possibly earlier. These early trails connected with existing (pre-European) foot routes that had been used by men and critters for thousands of years before that.

In Oregon the "Skyline Trail" ran from Mt. Hood to Crater Lake. Parts of this original trail still exist; some sections are paved over with modern roads, and other pieces were incorporated into today's PCT.

We can all be thankful that there were enough people of vision (and political will) to make this national treasure a reality. The Pacific Crest Trail was authorized by Congress in 1968 and dedicated in 1993; today's PCT stretches 2,650 miles from Mexico to Canada.

Oregon Backroads Guide to the Pacific Crest Trail

Suddenly, I found myself arriving at the enlightened age of 15. From this lofty pinnacle, I decided the words "cool" and "Boy Scouts" didn't go together. With my interests shifting more towards a cute red-haired girl who thought khaki green wasn't a proper color for me, the Scouts and I took different paths.

But this concept of a high country trail following the Pacific Divide continued to intrigue me. Wow… to strap your home on your back and hike from Mexico to Canada would truly be a worthy goal. Some hardy souls even do it in one season. I've seen claims that fewer people have thru-hiked the PCT in one season than have climbed Mt. Everest (nearly 4,000 people have achieved the summit of Mt. Everest as of late 2012).

In 1969 I entertained the thought that someday I would backpack from Mexico to Canada along the completed Pacific Crest Trail.

FAST FORWARD

OK, let's fast forward to the present….I'm thankful that I've lived in the beautiful Pacific Northwest…Washington, Alaska, and now Oregon, for over 40 years. I've been fortunate to have the time and health to explore on foot vast areas of pristine backcountry in the Pacific Northwest. I've hiked long stretches of the Pacific Crest Trail in Washington, Oregon, and California, but I've resigned myself to the fact that I'll never hike the PCT trail from end to end in one season (or probably one lifetime). Yes, life is full of little disappointments.

I'm not ready to hang up the hiking and camping gear though! I still crave time in the mountains and enjoy them in all seasons. The sweet rush of wind through the mountain treetops sings to me, and given the choice… I'll take the "scenic route" every time (thanks for the genes, Dad).

Of course now, instead of hoisting the butt-kicking, 70-lb. pack with my home and food for a week on board, we're more likely to go camping with the big tent, folding cot, propane stove, ice chest, maybe some beers, good food, wine, etc…in other words, the practical car camping outfit.

Introduction: A Twisting Journey

If the surrounding area is interesting, we can easily provision "base camp" for several days and then day hike from there. Or, quickly break camp and move on if the wind blows us another way…

After moving to southwestern Oregon in 2002, I started to explore my new high country backyard. Looking at the local map to see the direction the **Pacific Crest Trail** takes **as it enters Oregon from California**, I noted an interesting road route that closely follows the trail as it travels east across the crest of the **Siskiyou Mountains**. My first tentative trip into these mountains whetted my appetite for more. The Pacific Crest Trail winds its way through a series of 7,000-foot-plus peaks as it heads east towards its connection with the upstart **Cascade Mountains**.

THE LAY OF THE LAND

Oregon has always been a difficult place to get around in. Because of the rather orderly north-south nature of the Cascade Mountains, travelers from the east, heading towards the Pacific Ocean will be confronted with this natural barrier.

In the Cascades, several passes (low spots) present themselves to the traveler. These natural east-west trails were well established foot paths for thousands of years before Europeans arrived on the scene. In sharp contrast to the ordered structure of the Cascade Range, the jumbled geography of the Klamath and Siskiyou Mountains of southern Oregon makes travel (in any direction!) especially tough.

The **Siskiyou Range** is technically part of the geologically diverse **Klamath Mountains** of southern Oregon and northern California. The Siskiyous are a rarity in North American geography. Most mountains on this continent (like the Cascades) lie along a north-south axis. The Siskiyou Mountains run basically east-west, connecting with the (geologically young) Southern Oregon Cascades, southeast of Ashland, Oregon and the ancient (more than 400 million years old) Klamath Mountains to the west. This connection provides for a rich biological/geological diversity here.

Oregon Backroads Guide to the Pacific Crest Trail

Distant Mt. McLoughlin, a volcano in the Cascade Range, frames the horizon from the Siskiyou Crest.

The World Wildlife Fund has characterized this meeting place of the Siskiyou Range and the Cascades as the **"Galapagos of North America."** This is largely due to the fact that these mountains became an "island" during the last ice age (which ended around 11,500 years ago). They didn't suffer the heavy glaciations that carved the mountains just north of here. The plants and animals that evolved in the surrounding regions found refuge from the ice and largely survived here, today forming a unique community of plants and animals. To say the least, a marvelous melding of pretty juicy stuff…

Part of the Siskiyou Range (east of I-5) was recently designated as the **Soda Mountain Wilderness Area**, which is now part of the larger **Cascade-Siskiyou National Monument**. All of the Siskiyou Range would be designated as a National Park if it was east of the Mississippi River (and we would probably be busy loving it to death).

The high saddles and ridges of the Siskiyou Divide are among the most accessible in the region due to the existence of Forest

Introduction: A Twisting Journey

Service Road #20. Straddling the Rogue and Klamath drainages with stunning views in all directions and the southern horizon dominated by the awesome presence of California's Mt. Shasta, this road is definitely worth the trip. On a clear day it's certainly among the most "scenic routes" on the west coast of the United States. Yep, my new backyard is pretty cool.

Some time ago I started thinking about traveling the length of Oregon. **Shadowing the Pacific Crest Trail, I would seek out the "scenic route."** Traveling the backroads and staying in the high country would be my mantra. Keeping a journal along the way would be part of the fun too. Following the PCT from the point where it enters Oregon from the south (just like thru-hikers on the PCT do) all the way to the Columbia River and Washington State in the north would be my ultimate goal.

Of course the "research" involved in exploring a road trip version of the Pacific Crest Trail through Oregon would mean I would have an excuse for doing some of the things I love best. Lucky me….

WHY THIS GUIDE IS USEFUL

Those who choose to hike the Pacific Crest Trail would find it impossible to hike the length of it without support of friends, family, and those folks (trail angels) they'll meet along the way. To complete the journey, the hiker must rely on planned points along the trail where food and supplies can be shipped ahead (often by UPS) for later pick up.

The *Oregon Backroads Guide* is useful to pinpoint the places where roads intersect the PCT. My experience while researching this guide has shown that many friends and relatives of distance hikers drive ahead to pre-designated rendezvous points, providing material and psychological support for hikers. The *Oregon Backroads Guide* maps show roads near the PCT in easy-to-follow, color-coded routes. This information should also be useful to those who hike the trail in segments.

Plenty of words have already been written regarding the Pacific Crest Trail and this guide doesn't attempt to add to

Floating adventures are encouraged with descriptions of many lakes of significant size.

these excellent descriptions. I've included some day-hike trail descriptions to waterfalls and lakes along the road route, but I'll leave it up to the trail experts to describe the Pacific Crest Trail.

I hope the descriptions, maps, and photographs contained in the *Oregon Backroads Guide* will inspire everyone to explore and enjoy this beautiful and endlessly interesting land that surrounds us. Time spent in those places we love connects us to that land. Whether it's the oceans, the deserts, or the mountains, all of us on this journey can help protect the wild places that are left and preserve that legacy for those travelers yet to come.

If you have a small boat, a car topper, or inflatable, opportunities abound for floating adventures. The *Guide* describes many lakes, including Oregon's largest lake, and the headwaters of southern Oregon's most famous rivers. Even the first section through the Siskiyous has choice water features on both ends: the Applegate River and Emigrant Lake.

Introduction: A Twisting Journey

The other regions described in this guide feature an amazing assortment of glacier-carved alpine lakes and streams. The canoe-kayak trail along the northwestern shore of Upper Klamath Lake stands out among many great places to explore for the adventurous or those who just want to enjoy high country sun, earth, and water.

Of course, there are many opportunities for hiking and camping adventures along the way as well.

HOW TO USE THIS GUIDE

⇨ *This guide is designed to be a supplement to your map.*

Anyone who has traveled the backroads of Oregon can tell you what a challenge it can be. Many maps are lacking in detail, and the traveler quickly learns after leaving the pavement that the confusing maze of roads in the real world can be different than what a map shows.

New roads are added and old roads de-commissioned. Attempts at signage over time come and go. Signs sometimes are flat out lies, missing, or SUBAR (Shot Up Beyond All Recognition).

The *Backroads Guide* provides color-coded maps to help guide the traveler along the general route and through key intersections. These maps are numbered starting with the Region number followed by the map number. For example:

- Map number R3.3 would refer to Region Three, map 3
- Map number R2.1 would be Region Two, map 1 and the first in the Region Two series.

Make sure and bring your own map too.

As any good guide should be, this is definitely a work in progress. I've attempted to be as accurate as possible but know my efforts fall well short of perfection. I would ask the readers and users of this work to contact me with suggestions and corrections at ewmcb40@gmail.com.

Each region in this guide opens with:

Route Description: Provides a general description of the roads we'll be traveling.

Road Conditions: Describes clearance and traction issues along with vehicle recommendations and notes on seasonal closures.

Maps of the Area: Includes phone numbers by region for area Ranger Stations as well as info for obtaining needed maps on-line.

Main Roads in Order of Travel: A primary table provides a description of each road.

Optional and Secondary Roads: A secondary table provides a description and road number for optional routes.

Road Notes: These notes describe what to expect along the way including scenery, wildlife, history, restaurants/bars, groceries/gas, lodging, resorts/camping, hiking/fishing, and more.

BE PREPARED! *(Wisdom from an old Boy Scout)*

Just a few words about safety and etiquette when traveling the backroads:

- **Consider the season** and the weather when planning a trip in the high country.
- **Inquire locally** before traveling through snow country. Contact local Ranger Stations (phone numbers listed by region in the guide) for info on local road conditions.

Some storms can dump several feet of snow in a single blast, and then the weather may turn off dry and sunny for weeks at a time. It's not unusual to see several feet of snow on the ground at any time in the late fall through early spring at high elevations in the Siskiyous and Cascades.

Predicting weather is regarded by some as more of a sport than a science. Now that we've got satellites in space, meteorologists have a more than an even chance of getting it right. Pay atten-

Introduction: A Twisting Journey

tion to the weather forecast, and you'll sometimes find the most beautiful days in the mountains are in the late fall and early winter. This is especially true when the typical wintertime high pressure temperature inversions trap colder air and pollutants in the valleys below, leaving the higher terrain sunny and warm.

- **Be careful with fire!** The woods can be critically dry in the mountains of Oregon during the summer and fall. A bucket and shovel are a good idea. Don't ignore fire warnings, and only start campfires in existing fire rings.

- **Practice good etiquette.** Traveling as lightly as possible across the land should be our goal. This means leaving a minimum footprint. Much of this route is through high country with thin soils and short growing seasons. Avoid driving off established roads and respect wetlands. Please be sure to pick up your own trash and pitch in to pick up after those less considerate.

- **Fill your gas tank** where you can! Just do it… Plan to use more fuel per mile on back roads. Your vehicle works at consistently lower gears because you're at altitude and going slower. When traveling off the beaten path, gas stations (and grocery stores) can be few and far between.

- **Allow extra time.** Most regional routes described are less than 100 miles and can be traveled (rushed through) in less time than the *Guide* recommends. However, much of the route is along the backroads with less than perfect driving conditions (not a freeway) and plenty of places to explore. Create the opportunity to stop and smell the wildflowers!

- **Obtain maps of the area.** This guide references Forest Service maps found at your friendly Ranger Station, but look for maps on-line too. Very useful on-line tools for navigating available USGS maps can be found at store.usgs.gov. This site will direct you to a free Adobe add-on called "terraGo." Install this program to get all of the available features including the ability to download and use in your portable devices. Zoom in on the area you want and download the quad maps for free.

Oregon Backroads Guide to the Pacific Crest Trail

Another useful map is the *Oregon Road and Recreation Atlas* published by Benchmark Maps and available at your local outdoor goods retailer. This has the entire set of Oregon maps laid out in logical fashion along with tons of useful general information. I never venture forth without the atlas.

- **Bring water and food.** One gallon per person/per beast/per day is a good idea. Don't forget the groceries.
- **Pack blankets, sleeping bags, and warm clothes.** Yes, even in August! The high country is, well…high, and that means changeable weather and potential for cold temps any time of the year.

A HANDY CHECKLIST OF ITEMS TO CONSIDER
☐ Tent/Ground Pad
☐ Warm Clothes/Blanket
☐ Water/Food
☐ Rain Jacket
☐ First Aid Kit
☐ Flashlight and Batteries
☐ Matches/Lighter/Candle
☐ Knife
☐ Hatchet/Axe/Folding Saw
☐ Spade Tip Shovel (the most useful shape for most purposes)
☐ Jumper Cables/Spare Ignition Key
☐ Chains during Snow Season
☐ Small Tarp and at Least 50 Ft. of Stout Rope
☐ Sun Block/Insect Repellent/Toilet Paper
☐ Folding Chairs/Sunglasses/Binoculars
☐ Dishes and Utensils
☐ Camp Stove/Ice Chest
☐ Camera
☐ Towels

Introduction: A Twisting Journey

Do you need all this stuff? Probably not, but just like flood insurance, that day when the water starts rushing in, it's all worth it. I keep most of these items in an extra large duffel bag, ready to toss in the car.

BAD FEELINGS

⇨ *If you ever get one of these, stop and listen to your visceral self. Don't freak out; assess your options. Turn back if you have serious doubts.*

Is the snow piling up and the hour getting late? Don't hesitate to turn around before the snow gets too deep to do so easily. Certain all-wheel-drive vehicles (like a Subaru Outback) have just enough clearance and traction to get your ass in serious trouble when it becomes high centered. Your big snarly, gas hoggy SUV or pick-up (like a Toyota Tundra) can often travel even further up the mountain before high centering, so let's not be smug, eh?

Sometimes though, trouble comes in other forms. For instance, is your spare tire inflated? I'm not even going to ask if you have a jack and tire wrench...

Another good way to get yourself in trouble is relying on your GPS (Global Positioning System). Although these devices are becoming more sophisticated, some serious high profile mishaps involving lost families have forced manufacturers to be more careful with "shortcut directions."

Google Maps supplied with most smart phones are remarkably accurate on the larger scale, but often questionable on a smaller scale. Off the beaten path, your smart phone is definitely useful where you can get reception (or the stupid battery isn't dead), but don't rely on that alone.

The best problem solving device you have is your brain. It's also the best tool for staying out of trouble to begin with. If you make one bad decision and compound it with another one, things can start rolling downhill in a hurry.

Dealing with trouble in the back country can often mean dealing with it alone. AAA probably isn't sending a locksmith into the back country to make an ignition key or jump a dead car battery, especially after you just lost your cell phone in the river!

Introduction: A Twisting Journey

A FEW WORDS ABOUT VEHICLES

With a few exceptions, the majority of this route can be done in any vehicle with a short wheelbase and reasonable clearance. **Where clearance and traction are an issue, I have provided alternate routes.**

Of course, traveling as lightly as possible has its virtues beyond better gas mileage and a shorter turning radius. A smaller passenger car (let's call it a pre-2004 Toyota Camry for reference) has greater range and overall leaves a smaller footprint on the land but may have clearance and traction issues. All of the paved roads and most of the gravel roads described in this guide are great for this vehicle in good weather.

Other short wheelbase, two-wheel drive vehicles (let's call it a bright yellow Ford Ranger pick-up) can often go places where a passenger car can't. Usually clearance is more of an issue than traction in good weather.

This route is perfectly suited in good weather to the new generation of mid-size "crossover" SUVs with all-wheel drive (let's call it a Subaru Outback with a luggage rack for reference). This type of vehicle offers a nice compromise between clearance, gas mileage, and traction.

Your big snarly, gas hoggy, four-wheel drive SUV or pick-up (let's call it a Chevy Tahoe with custom wheels) has lots of room for the family and gear and has all the clearance and traction you'll probably ever need to ford a river or scale a mountain — but when was the last time you needed to do that? Needless to say, in good weather, none of the road descriptions contained within this guide are beyond the capabilities of such vehicles.

Explore, enjoy, and wave (at least lift your little finger off the steering wheel) to your fellow travelers!

The freedom of the hills calls to me. And so I must go.

— *Ed W. McBee, June 11th, 2013*

No squeaky toys were harmed in the making of this book.

ABOUT THE AUTHOR

Ed McBee has always had a love for the high country. Traveling the mountains of the Cascades, Siskiyous, and Sierras, Ed has explored some of the most beautiful and remote landscapes in the west, afoot, afloat, and a-wheeled.

After moving to the Seattle area from the plains of Kansas as he turned 15, Ed commenced to poke and prod every corner of the Pacific Northwest from Alaska to California, at one time dreaming of hiking the 2,650 mile length of the Pacific Crest Trail from Mexico to Canada.

Now residing in southern Oregon, Ed owns a business in the Historic Landmark District of Jacksonville. His sidekick Brio is a cowdog without cows who rides shotgun when they're exploring the backroads of Oregon and corrals squeaky toys in Ed's office.

REGION ONE
Jacksonville to Emigrant Lake

The Applegate Valley has become a beacon for winemakers. Some of the oldest vines in the area are at Valley View Winery.

"Instead of goin' to Heaven, they went to Jacksonville."
— Lyle Lovett

High country adventure is a short drive from the historic town of Jacksonville, the starting point for Region One.

Region 1 — Jacksonville to Emigrant Lake

ROUTE DESCRIPTION

Our journey begins in the southwestern Oregon town of Jacksonville. After driving south through the beautiful Applegate Valley, we'll pick up the Pacific Crest Trail as it enters Oregon from California and then follows Forest Service Road #20 along the crest of the Siskiyou Mountains. The Region One route ends at Emigrant Lake near Ashland, Oregon. Total road miles are 60–75; optional roads are included in the larger figure.

⇨ **Allow 6 hours with stops.**
⇨ **Jacksonville is the last reliable place to fuel up.**

ROAD CONDITIONS

Mostly paved and improved gravel, some rough road and clearance issues are along the Siskiyou Crest Road. The route is OK for two-wheel drive vehicles with clearance in good weather (let's call it a Toyota Tacoma two-wheel-drive pick-up with faded blue paint for comparison). It is better-suited for your Subaru Outback/SUV all-wheel drive and up.

Because of the high elevation along the Siskiyou Crest Road (over 7,000 ft. in spots), Forest Service Road #20 is typically closed by snow until early summer. Other state highways and paved county roads described in Region One are plowed in the winter months.

MAPS FOR THIS AREA

Both the Rogue River and the Applegate maps are available at the Applegate District Office (the Star Ranger Station). Order maps on-line at fs.usda.gov/rogue-siskiyou. For info on Region One road conditions call 541-899-3800. Find Benchmark Maps at your local sporting goods store or benchmarkmaps.com.

- *Rogue River National Forest Visitors Map*
- Applegate & West Half of Ashland Ranger Districts Map
- Benchmark Maps – *Oregon Road and Recreation Atlas* – pages 96 and 97

MAIN ROADS IN ORDER OF TRAVEL

All Regional Routes are listed South to North.

Hwy. 238	West from Jacksonville to the town of Ruch.
Upper Applegate Rd.	South from the town of Ruch to Beaver Creek Road.
Beaver Creek Rd.	This turns into FS Road #20 where the pavement ends.
Forest Rd. #20	Turns into County Road #1151 at Mt. Ashland.
Rd. #1151	The paved Mt. Ashland road connection to Old Hwy. 99.
Hwy. 99	The paved alternative to I-5, connects to Hwy. 66.
Hwy. 66	The paved road to the town of Ashland and Emigrant Lake.

OPTIONAL & SECONDARY ROADS

Roads are also described in the Road Notes.

FS Rd. #2025	Connects with the #20 Road at Silver Fork Gap. Goes to Donomore Meadows.
Rd. #40S01	The "scenic route" back to the #20 Road at Jackson Gap from Donomore Meadows.
Rd. #805	The driveway to Dutchman Peak Lookout.
FS Rd. #22	A shorter road down from Siskiyou Summit Road (#20) to I-5.

Region 1 — Jacksonville to Emigrant Lake

MAP R1.1: MAIN ROUTE

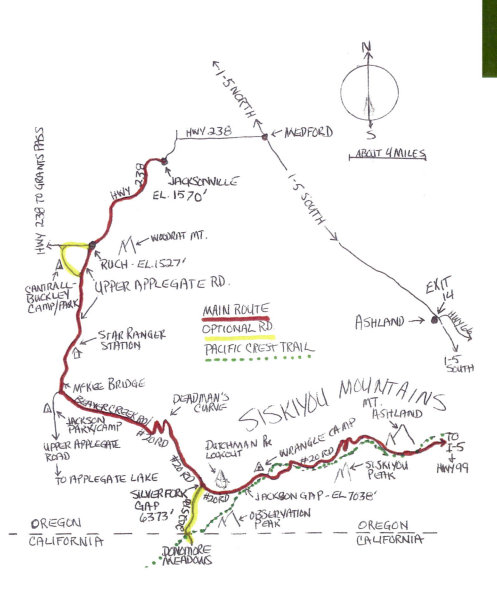

After a series of fires, the town of Jacksonville rebuilt using bricks.

ROAD NOTES — REGION ONE

Starting in Jacksonville, the following notes give details about the sights, history, and attractions along the way.

JACKSONVILLE: Elevation 1,570 ft.
From Jacksonville we head west on Hwy. 238 to Ruch.

The **"National Historic Landmark District"** of Jacksonville (one of 18 so designated historical landmarks in the State of Oregon) is an attractive gold rush town situated in southern Oregon. Located west of Medford along the I-5 corridor, it was once the Jackson County seat (now moved to Medford since 1927) and one of the few significant mining towns that survived from boom times to modern times. After a series of fires, many of the downtown buildings were rebuilt using brick. The town survived hard times through the Depression after the railroad passed it by and was revitalized starting in the 1960s.

Jacksonville is well worth a closer examination of the four to five square blocks making up the Historic Landmark District. Consisting of several residences and government buildings,

Region 1 — Jacksonville to Emigrant Lake

including the old courthouse, city hall, and jail, the downtown core also has a thriving commercial district with interesting and eclectic shops, bars, and restaurants. Above town, a network of hiking trails is readily accessible with interpretive signs about the gold mining activities that took place here.

Jacksonville's location, ambiance, and sunny climate certainly lend credence to those who say that this town is evolving into the hub of the rapidly expanding wine industry of southern Oregon and the nearby Applegate Valley. Get to know some great local wines at **South Stage Cellars** tasting room, located near the corner of 3rd and California Streets. Several other regional winemakers offer their wares around Jacksonville.

The World of Wine Festival has become an annual event in Jacksonville and is a showcase of local wines and foodie events. For more information look on the web at worldofwinefestival.com.

Many of the businesses along California Street work the history angle of the town into their image. The vintage **Jacksonville**

Completed in 1854, St. Andrew's Anglican Church on 5th Street was the first Protestant church built west of the Rockies.

Barber Shop is the oldest continually operating business in town, offering old-time service with modern style. The barber, widely acknowledged as an expert on all things, is also a good source for local information.

Just across the street from the barber shop, ask for the thin crust pizza at the Italian-themed (with a western flair) **Bella Union Restaurant and Saloon**. Check out the giant wisteria covering the back patio.

The **Boomtown Saloon**, also located on California Street, has food (try the sausage dog) a decent pool table, a shuffleboard, and a nice selection of Oregon beers. Several other restaurants and bars tucked into the historic district offer a range of dishes and beverages from upscale cuisine at the **Jacksonville Inn** to excellent Asian-influenced dishes at the local Thai restaurant.

During the summer, Jacksonville hosts the **Britt Musical Festival** (the Brittfest), a collection of diverse concerts in a beautiful hillside setting a couple of blocks above town. Held on the grounds of Peter Britt's estate, most concerts allow beer, wine,

The vintage Jacksonville Barber Shop is located in the center of the historic district. "Thanks Ed, it looks great..."

Region 1 — Jacksonville to Emigrant Lake

The back patio at the Bella Union is covered by a giant wisteria.

and food. Bring a blanket and some stubby-legged chairs and enjoy the often noteworthy talent. More information is available at brittfest.org.

Peter Britt was a Swiss emigrant and arrived in Jacksonville in 1852, shortly after gold was discovered. Trying his hand at gold prospecting, he soon turned to other enterprises including photography and winemaking. Britt was a pioneer in viticulture, experimenting with different grapes, along with fruit trees and ornamental plants to find what grew best in the surrounding area. Many of Britt's early photographs of the region survive today along with the first photos of Crater Lake, taken in 1874.

Jacksonville to Ruch: We head west on Highway 238. It's about 7.3 miles to the Upper Applegate Road turnoff.

As we follow Highway 238 west out of Jacksonville towards the town of Ruch (pronounced "roosh"), the highway at first follows Jackson Creek. Heading uphill on Highway 238 and glancing to the right, we see remnants (now a gated quarry) of the gold mining activity that took place here mostly in the last half of the 19th century. Just out of town on our left is a

Oregon Backroads Guide to the Pacific Crest Trail

The Britt Festival entrance is a pleasant stroll past the Britt Gardens.

parking lot and trailhead for the "Britt Trails." The trails are also named after Peter Britt.

Cresting **Jacksonville Hill** (elevation 2,615 ft.), we're officially in the Applegate River drainage. We pass through farm and woodlands as we head west on Highway 238. As we approach Ruch, looking to our left, we see Woodrat Mountain. The clearings located on the upper slopes are launching pads for paragliders taking advantage of local thermal updrafts. Paraglider pilots travel here from around the world to participate in an annual gliding competition called **Star Thistle**. For more information on Star Thistle look on-line at rvhpa.org

At 7.3 miles from Jacksonville we come to the town of Ruch.

RUCH: Elevation 1,527 ft.
From Ruch we'll turn south on Upper Applegate Road.

Ruch is the commercial and residential center for this part of the beautiful **Applegate Valley**. Along with a couple of small cafés and garden stores catering to the burgeoning herbal farmers of the valley, there's a well-stocked grocery store.

Region 1 — *Jacksonville to Emigrant Lake*

MAP R1.2: JACKSONVILLE TO SILVER FORK GAP

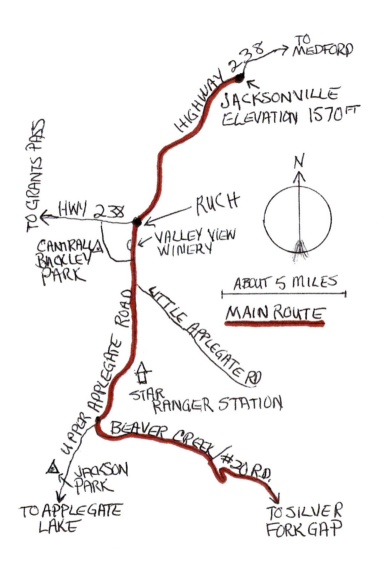

You'll also find a visitors center with information on nearby camping at **Cantrell-Buckley Park**, the growing number of local wineries, and many other local events and attractions.

Upper Applegate Road to Beaver Creek Road: It's about 8.6 miles from Ruch to our next turnoff at Beaver Creek Road.

The Upper Applegate Road heads south from Ruch, passes through the residential area of town, and then opens up to acres of vineyards adjacent to the tasting rooms of **Valley View Winery**. Stop in, meet the friendly staff, and sample the excellent local wines. From here look south and view the mountains of the western Siskiyous.

Heading south again on Upper Applegate Road, our next destination is the Star Ranger Station, about 6.1 miles from Ruch.

Star Ranger Station: Call 541-899-3800 for Region One road information. The Ranger Station sells an excellent map of the Region One area. Titled **Applegate and West Half of the Ashland Ranger Districts**, it's a highly detailed topo map (1 inch = 1 mile) of the high Siskiyous and well worth the $6 price. The

Valley View Winery's tasting room offers delectable wine samples and a delicious view of their acres of vineyards.

Region 1 — Jacksonville to Emigrant Lake

This big kitty greets visitors at the Star Ranger Station.

station is open Monday through Friday or order on-line at fs.usda.gov/rogue-siskiyou.

Just inside the door to the Ranger Station lobby there's a stuffed mountain lion on display. If I wanted to give my cow-dog Brio a thrill (and I don't), I'd put him on a leash for a tour. Yes, it's OK with the staff and it might be worth a YouTube video of your dog's reaction…

Heading south again on Upper Applegate Road, our next waypoint is the **Historic McKee Covered Bridge**, about 8.0 miles south of Ruch.

The McKee Covered Bridge is among the oldest of the surviving covered bridges in Oregon and was built in 1917. One of the few remaining covered bridges in this part of southern Oregon, it's also among the highest covered bridges at around 39 feet. At one time it was an important crossing on this part of the Applegate River and was originally constructed to run trucks filled with copper ore from the now abandoned **Blue Ledge Mine**.

The historic McKee Covered Bridge on the Applegate River originally was used for bringing copper ore from the Blue Ledge Mine.

Closed now for decades to vehicular traffic, the bridge was recently (October 2011) closed to foot traffic. Currently, some groups of bridge and history buffs are working with county officials to restore and secure the bridge for future generations.

The **McKee Bridge Restaurant and Bar** attaches to the modest general store just before the day-use area and historic covered bridge. Stop in for fried chicken and chips, plus local gossip. The folks at the store are a good source for local road information.

Still heading south on the Upper Applegate Road, **keeping left at the "Y,"** we cross the Applegate River at 8.3 miles from Ruch. After going over the bridge look for the **second road to your left**, 8.6 miles from Ruch, this is the Beaver Creek Road and the continuation of the Main Route (marked red on Map R1.2).

> ⇨ **Special Note:** *A pleasant campground, called Jackson Park, is just a half-mile south from the Beaver Creek intersection. Stay on the Upper Applegate Road, heading south towards Applegate Lake.*

Region 1 — Jacksonville to Emigrant Lake

The upper Applegate River runs crystal clear and cold.

Jackson Park and Campground is situated between Upper Applegate Road and the cold, clear Applegate River. Watch for water ouzels and belted kingfishers here. This is a good place to splash around with a beautiful gravel beach and plenty of shallow places for children to wade in the summer. The park is a good place to fish during the winter steelhead season. The campsites are a little tightly spaced with no hook-ups. This fee area has water, toilets, and a day-use area. For information and reservations, call 541-899-9220 or look on-line at apple-gatelake.com.

BEAVER CREEK INTERSECTION: Elevation 1,670 ft. The Main Route (marked red on the Map R1.2) heads east on Beaver Creek Road.

Beaver Creek Road turns into Forest Service Road #20 where the pavement ends, 5.5 miles ahead. The sign points east towards Dutchman Peak Lookout and Mt. Ashland. We'll stay on this road for the next 13.2 miles to a five-way intersection known as **Silver Fork Gap**.

Beaver Creek Road to Silver Fork Gap:
Beaver Creek Road heads east-southeast 5.5 miles before turning to gravel and becoming FS Road #20. About a mile past the pavement we are officially in the Rogue River National Forest. Some twists in the road ahead are named "Deadman's Curve" so be prepared for some steep grades, washboards, and sharp corners; but this road is doable in any vehicle. The road heads steadily up and south.

At about 10.1 miles we pass the intersection of the #2015/ **Maple Dell Road** on our right. Stay left, heading uphill on the #20 Road. At 10.5 miles, views to the west reveal the peaks of the western Siskiyous and the **Red Buttes Wilderness**.

At 13.2 miles from the Upper Applegate Road we arrive at the nicely named **Silver Fork Gap**. A "gap" in this sense is just a low spot in the Siskiyou Range, a "pass" or "saddle." The "Silver Fork" part refers to the Silver Fork branch of Elliot Creek, which heads near here and flows into the Applegate River just above Applegate Lake, far to our west.

Look for the peaks of the Red Buttes Wilderness along this part of the #20 Road.

Region 1 — Jacksonville to Emigrant Lake

MAP R1.3: SILVER FORK GAP OPTIONS

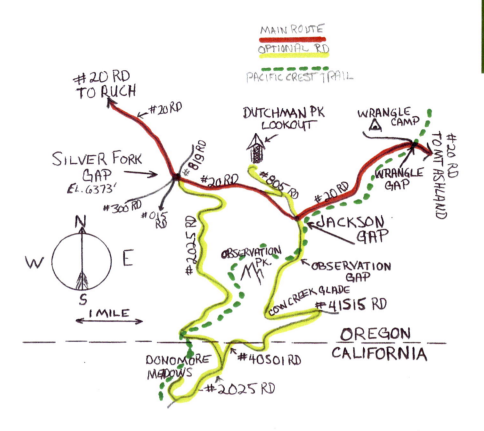

This map illustrates the options we have from Silver Fork Gap. The PCT enters Oregon just north of beautiful Donomore Meadows and edges north around 7,340 ft. Observation Peak. Cow Creek Glade (also known as the Observation Peak Botanical Area) is tucked into the eastern flank of this mountain. Dutchman Peak Lookout is nearby on the #805 Road.

SILVER FORK GAP INTERSECTION: Elevation 6,373 ft.

⇨ **Special Note:** *There are two options from here; both are described below. This is a 5-way intersection. Facing south, the first road to your left, Road #819, is a short road that heads further uphill to a quarry with a nice spot for rustic camping in the adjacent forest. The next road to your left and heading east is FS Road #20 to Mt. Ashland.*

⇨ *Having trouble orienting? Since we arrived at this intersection pointing south, flip the Silver Fork Gap Map 180 degrees and orient the North arrow toward the road we came in on.*

FIRST OPTION
Main Route: The Main Route turns east on FS Road #20 (this is the red route marked on the Silver Fork Gap map) toward nearby Jackson Gap (about 2 miles). From Silver Fork Gap, the #20 Road narrows and heads sharply uphill to Jackson Gap after passing the #805 Road to **Dutchman Peak Lookout.** The #20 Road gets better at **Jackson Gap.**

Built in 1927, Dutchman Peak Lookout is a "cupola style" fire lookout that is still staffed in the summer.

Region 1 — Jacksonville to Emigrant Lake

DUTCHMAN PEAK LOOKOUT: Elevation 7,417 ft.
⇨ **Not recommended for passenger cars.**

Dutchman Peak is worth checking out just for the incredible 360-degree view. The handicap accessible vault toilet is just frosting on the giant cupcake. Located near the lookout at 7,368 ft., it's guaranteed among the highest facilities in Oregon and open to the public!

This outhouse could provide you with your own "private" viewpoint if you prop the door open with a rock. Truly a peak experience, and so is the lookout. The road up to the peak is a little steep and rocky; the leg of the driveway from Jackson Gap is the best way. Just below the lookout cabin at the switchback, the road gets a little worse at a turnaround. Park here if needed and walk the short way to the summit.

Heading down the road from Dutchman Peak, stay left at the "Y," and you're at **Jackson Gap Intersection**. (See below for a description of Jackson Gap Intersection.)

SECOND OPTION
Silver Fork Gap to Donomore Meadow: Head south on the #2025 Road to Donomore Meadow (this is the Yellow route marked on the Map R1.3: Silver Fork Gap), the optional Cow Creek Glade loop, and back to Jackson Gap.

On the south side of the Silver Fork intersection is the #2025 Road. Otherwise **unmarked**, a sign here (as of 7/11/13) indicates that this road is closed 23 miles ahead. Heading downhill, this road takes us to **Donomore Meadow** and the point where the PCT enters Oregon from California.

The payoff for traveling the #2025 Road a few miles south from here are big views of Mt. Shasta, the Klamath Mountains, and the endless mountains to the southwest. The #2025 Road intersects the Pacific Crest Trail at 3.8 miles (elevation 6,238 ft.) south of Silver Fork Gap, just above Donomore Meadows. Past this point the big juicy views of Mt. Shasta begin. At 4.6 miles from Silver Fork Gap, gaze down to your right into beautiful Donomore Meadows. On the left side (south) of the

Region 1 — Jacksonville to Emigrant Lake

meadow is a pleasant campsite adjacent to some big trees... See anybody there? At this point you've entered the Golden State of California.

At 4.8 miles from Silver Fork Gap the #2025 Road intersects the **#40S01 Road** to the left. This is the optional "scenic" route back to the #20 Road at Jackson Gap via the Cow Creek Glade Loop. (See complete route description for the #40S01 Road below).

Just past this intersection, and still heading south on the #2025 Road, an informational sign indicates that Donomore Meadow is 2 miles ahead. According to my odometer however, **the turnoff to the meadow is almost exactly one mile from this sign**. After traveling the mile, take the second downhill road to the right (north). Stay left at the "Y" to explore the meadows (there's a turnaround at this spot). Some erosion has caused ruts here; park and walk the rest of the way if the road is muddy. It's about 0.2 miles further downhill to the campsite (elevation 5,700 ft.) we spied from above.

Donomore Meadow: The PCT edges along the southwest side of this serene, high country meadow as it heads toward the Oregon state line to the northeast. Check out the wooden foot bridge over Donomore Creek. Look for the remains (mostly crushed by the heavy snows) of an old shepherd's cabin near the PCT on the north side of the meadow.

In the summer months the meadow is alive with wildflowers, blacktail deer, soaring hawks, and the occasional free range cow...Look (and listen at night) for owls in the adjacent woods.

Heading out of the meadow and back to the #2025 Road, we'll turn left (uphill) and drive **back the way we came in**.

In just over one mile from Donomore we're back to the intersection with the #40S01 Road. Those drivers with more capable vehicles may wish to take the #40S01 Road back to Forest Service Road #20 and Jackson Gap, via stunning **Cow**

⇐   The PCT bridge crosses over Donomore Creek as it meanders through the meadow.

Oregon Backroads Guide to the Pacific Crest Trail

Creek Glade. (See full description of the optional #40S01 Road intersection below). Everyone else keeps heading north (the way we came in) on the #2025 Road, 4.8 miles back to Silver Fork Gap.

Turn right (east) from Silver Fork Gap onto the #20 Road towards Mt. Ashland. The first road we encounter to our left is the #805 Road, the driveway up to Dutchman Peak Lookout. A short way past this we come to Jackson Gap Intersection. (See below for Jackson Gap Intersection description.)

#40S01 ROAD INTERSECTION: Elevation 6,193 ft.
⇨ **Not recommended for passenger cars.**

This is the optional "Scenic Route" back to Jackson Gap and the #20 Road via **Cow Creek Glade**.

Narrow in spots but not really steep, its about 4.3 miles total via the #40S01 Road back to the #20 Road. There are some clearance issues. No problem in your Subaru Outback and up (in good weather) but I don't recommend this road for passenger cars.

Numerous springs support lush gardens at Cow Creek Glade.

Region 1 — Jacksonville to Emigrant Lake

Serpentine, formed in deep ocean subduction zones, is now deposited at over 6,000 feet in the Siskiyous.

This intersection is situated on the ridge dividing the Rogue River drainage from the Klamath River drainage. Walk a few yards west from the intersection and gaze down into the Applegate River drainage. Look along the shallow depression carved into the ground here and admire the huge boulders of **serpentine rock** strewn about.

Serpentine is formed in deep ocean subduction zones, created when the water is squeezed out of the heavier sea floor as it is forced (in an on-going process) beneath the lighter continental plates and combines with mantle rocks. Called serpentine because of its greenish, scaly appearance, these rocks are polished by the pressure and movement inherent in subduction zones. High in magnesium but lacking in elements that support plant growth, areas of serpentine are often treeless with only a scattering of hardy grass and small shrubs to be seen.

With big vistas of California mountains waiting around every corner, the #40S01 Road edges along the southern flanks of **Observation Peak** (elevation 7,340 ft.) and crosses the Oregon state line in about 0.5 miles.

Oregon Backroads Guide to the Pacific Crest Trail

At the Jackson Gap intersection, Dutchman Peak is the highest point on the left. The road to the right goes to Mt. Ashland.

In 2.1 miles we come to the intersection of the **#41S15 Road** where we will keep to the left (west). At 2.6 miles we pass the #48N21 Road on our right.

Continue straight (uphill) on the #40S01 Road. Soon we enter the verdant and inelegantly named **Cow Creek Glade** (also called the **Observation Peak Botanical Area**), a magical rock garden of high country plants and animals.

Park at the head of the glade and soak up the scenery. Cow Creek is fed by multiple springs and flows northeast. Look far to the east and see the Doppler radar dome perched atop Mt. Ashland. Tread lightly as you explore on foot the fragile flower gardens and miniature waterfalls adorning the hillside.

An old (closed to motorized vehicles) Jeep road heads up the southern flank of Observation Peak. Huff and puff your way up the hill, keeping to the right as you come to the ridgeline. Continue uphill and north to the first of the two summits atop Observation Peak. Look for the signs of old mining activity below the western side of the summit ridge.

Region 1 — Jacksonville to Emigrant Lake

The #40S01 Road intersects the PCT at 4.0 miles, elevation 7,028 feet. Just a quarter-mile past this we come to Jackson Gap and the #20 Road.

<u>JACKSON GAP INTERSECTION:</u> Elevation 7,038 ft. The Main Route heads east on the #20 Road.

At our feet to the south lies twin-topped **Observation Peak**, elevation 7,340 ft. This north-facing slope sometimes sports a healthy snowfield well into summer. When the snows are gone, it's a pretty easy hike up to the top; follow the PCT a couple of hundred yards west from its intersection with the #40S01 Road to the scree slope below the north summit. A short, steep scramble delivers you to the north summit. Remember to account for the high elevations when estimating hiking time in the Siskiyous.

Those who arrived here via Cow Creek Glade Road (the **second option**) and haven't been up to Dutchman Peak Lookout, now's your chance. The lookout lies just above this intersection.

Those of you who chose to come here directly from Silver Fork Gap (the **first option**), now's your chance to explore

Late spring wildflowers carpet the ground at Jackson Gap.

Oregon Backroads Guide to the Pacific Crest Trail

Lichens paint the rocks above Wrangle Gap. Mt. Shasta is in the distance.

Cow Creek Glade. OK for passenger cars, head south on the #40S01 Road about 1.2 miles and park at the head of the glade to explore the rock gardens.

Jackson Gap: It's just over 2.0 miles to **Wrangle Gap**. The #20 Road traverses the true crest of the Siskiyous, heading in a northeast direction. Shortly after leaving Jackson Gap we encounter the **Sheep Camp Springs Road** to our right. This is essentially a PCT hiker's camp and not a good car camp (brushy with a tight turnaround at the bottom).

The PCT is our constant companion from Jackson Gap to Wrangle Gap, paralleling the #20 Road to our right. We intersect the PCT at 2.0 miles and come to Wrangle Gap, 2.1 miles from Jackson Gap.

WRANGLE GAP INTERSECTION: Elevation 6,538 ft. We head east on the #20 Road from Wrangle Gap. It's 3.6 miles to Long John Saddle from Wrangle Gap.

Directly above us to the northeast is the unimaginatively named **Big Red Mountain**, elevation 7,064 ft. The Pacific Crest

Region 1 — Jacksonville to Emigrant Lake

Trail detours sharply north around Big Red Mountain while the #20 Road heads south and east to skirt the southern flanks. We'll meet up with the PCT again at **Siskiyou Gap**.

The road to our right (heading south into a maze of logging roads) is the #40S12 Road.

The road to our left (north) is the #2030 Road, leading a short way down to **Wrangle Camp**. This small campground is sheltered from the wind for the most part and a good place to take a break and look around. I don't recommend exploring the #2030 Road beyond the camp; it's steep, rocky, and brushy as it dives north down Wrangle Creek Canyon.

Wrangle Gap to Siskiyou Gap: It's 3.0 miles to Siskiyou Gap. Heading east from Wrangle Gap the #20 Road changes in nature, becoming rough and narrow in spots as it winds its way along the south side of Big Red Mountain. Take it easy and pick your way through the short uphill/downhill sections. Don't expect to make time on this section of the road in any vehicle. Cheer up though; this is the worst part of the whole road (almost).

Remember to take into account high elevations when estimating hiking time. We summited Mt. McDonald just before dusk.

There are a few good wide spots to park and admire the views along the way to Siskiyou Gap. Grab the folding chairs and binoculars as you take a break to watch the world go by.

This is also a good spot for bird watching. Certain rare, high altitude adapted species like the brightly colored **lazuli bunting**, and **mountain bluebirds** can occasionally be spotted in the nearby woods along with soaring birds almost at eye level.

SISKIYOU GAP INTERSECTION: Elevation 5,902 ft. From Siskiyou Gap we head east on the #20 Road. The PCT crosses here. It's 0.5 miles to **Long John Saddle** from Siskiyou Gap.

MAP R1.4: WRANGLE GAP TO MT. ASHLAND

Region 1 — Jacksonville to Emigrant Lake

To our right (south) lies the #40S12 Road, which leads down into more unmarked logging roads and drainages to the Klamath River.

Downslope to our left (north) are the **headwaters of the Little Applegate River**, a major tributary to the Applegate River and ultimately the Rogue River.

The #20 Road heads northeast from Siskiyou Gap (uphill) and skirts along the north side of the Siskiyou Divide. The views begin to change as we glimpse the volcanic cone of **Mt. McLoughlin** to the northeast. At 5.7 miles from Jackson Gap we come to Long John Saddle and an intersection with the PCT.

LONG JOHN SADDLE INTERSECTION:
Elevation 5,877 ft.

From Long John Saddle we head uphill and east on the #20 Road. The PCT crosses here. Consult Map R1.4.

At these elevations you just might need your long johns, eh?

This is a five-way intersection (a tangle of roads) with a lack of adequate signage. Look around in the trees and try to decipher

Make sure to take time to enjoy some great views.

Courtesy Dennis Kruse.

the words and numbers. There may be an informational sign indicating that Wrangle Gap is 5 miles back the way we came and **Grouse Gap** is 5 miles to the east. The **Grouse Gap/Mt. Ashland Road is the way to go; this is the #20 Road.**

There are two roads to our right (south) leading down to the maze of logging roads etched into the south slope of the Siskiyou Mountains, (Rds. #40S16 and #40S20).

The road to our left (north) is the #2040 Road and hooks up with the Little Applegate drainage. It's brushy and steep like most of the roads on the north side of the range. **Staying on the #20 Road heading uphill** and to the north we immediately come to another intersection with the #22 Road to our left.

The #22 Road is improved and is a quicker way back to Interstate 5 and civilization. Heading north and downhill, the #22 Road follows **Wagner Creek** to the town of **Talent** and I-5. If you want to bail out, this is your last chance to get back to early 21st century America without traversing the last 2.5 miles of rough road before **Grouse Gap** and **Mt. Ashland.**

For those of you in for the full tour, the #20 Road heads uphill from here as we edge along the north side of the Siskiyou divide.

Long John Saddle to Meridian Overlook: It's 2.5 miles to Meridian Overlook.

The #20 Road heads sharply north and uphill before turning abruptly east as we leave Long John Saddle. There are remnants of pavement along this section of road but don't expect a super highway. The way is rough and it's slow going but any vehicle will suffice with care.

Along the way we encounter big views to the north. Take a peek-a-boo look down into the valley of Bear Creek and the I-5 corridor as it snakes north. The volcanic silhouette of Mt. McLoughlin (elevation 9,495 ft.) looms to the northeast.

At 8.3 miles from Jackson Gap we come to the **Meridian Overlook** and the end of rough roads.

Region 1 — Jacksonville to Emigrant Lake

Siskiyou Peak is a short hike from Meridian Overlook.

MERIDIAN OVERLOOK: Elevation 6,890 ft.

Meridian Overlook (lying along the north-south Willamette Meridian) was once a developed way-point along the #20 Road with informational signs embedded in granite pedestals. Originally there were pictures here identifying the myriad mountain peaks on display to our south as well as info on the specialized plants and animals adapted to the Siskiyous. Too bad some cretins decided to vandalize this site.

The pedestals (arranged in an arc) are all that remain, lending it the air of a Druid ceremonial center. Those travelers who are of the "ceremonial" bent may wish to celebrate here…

Or… walk the (illegal) tire tracks that lead south and west, staying on the uphill side as you hook up with the **Pacific Crest Trail** to its high point below **Siskiyou Peak**. Take the obvious side trail from the PCT leading south and uphill. Look for rock cairns as you approach the summit rocks, trending to your left. Siskiyou Peak will reward your efforts with sweeping views of the surrounding country including a look-back at Cow Creek Glade, about 5.5 miles to the west.

If the weather's good and you have the time, I definitely recommend the hike. Better yet, toss a sandwich and some water in your rucksack and picnic on top of Siskiyou Peak (elevation 7,149 ft.). It's not far to the top but the high altitude will have you breathing a little harder by the time you get there.

Meridian Overlook is also a designated "Heli-Spot" sometimes used by search and rescue and firefighters.

Heading east again on the #20 Road, the PCT parallels our way on the south side of the road. Near here, at an unnamed saddle between Siskiyou Peak and McDonald Peak, a snow bank sometimes persists (in heavy snow years) until early July.

The #20 Road curves and twists its way eastward and just over 2.0 miles from Meridian Overlook we come to the **Grouse Gap Intersection**.

GROUSE GAP INTERSECTION: Elevation 6,453 ft. The #20 Road heads uphill and east. **The PCT crosses here.** Views to the south abound. Gaze at the (usually snow-capped) **Trinity Alps** to the west of **Mt. Shasta**.

The Grouse Gap shelter is a great place to park and explore.

Region 1 — Jacksonville to Emigrant Lake

The funny object on top of Mt. Ashland is a Doppler Radar station.

The ample shelter located a quarter-mile downhill is complete with an open fire-pit and chimney. A favorite destination of cross country skiers in the wintertime, in the warmer months this is a good place to park and explore beautiful Grouse Creek Glade.

Grouse Gap to Mt. Ashland Campground: It's about 1.7 miles to the campground. Continuing east on the #20 Road we soon encounter a secondary road angling uphill to our left. This is the access road to the Doppler radar station atop **Mt. Ashland**.

Mt. Ashland Summit Road: The road is a bit rough and I don't recommend it for passenger cars, but for those with more capable vehicles, take the 1.5 mile drive and soak up the amazing views atop Mt. Ashland. At 7,533 ft., this is the highest peak in the Siskiyous.

The 28-foot diameter "radome" houses a rotating radar dish that was installed in 1996 and upgraded with new technology in 2012 to better predict severe weather in the area. Back on the #20 Road still heading east, the PCT is on our right. We encounter the **Mt. Ashland Campground** at 12.0 miles from Jackson Gap.

MT. ASHLAND CAMPGROUND: Elevation 6,716 ft.

So you want to spend the night up here on the rooftop of southern Oregon? Now's your chance! One of the most spectacular campsites in Oregon, the views from here are exceptional on a clear day. With eight tent sites tucked into the hillside above and below the road, the campground has 2 toilets, picnic tables, and fire rings, but no water.

Grab your binoculars and gaze at the tiny-looking big rigs on I-5 (many miles away) as they pull the grade up to **Siskiyou Summit**. During the day take advantage of the many hiking opportunities in the area. Be sure and bring your field guides to identify the myriad birds, unique butterflies, and wildflowers that call these ridges home. At night around the campfire (bring your own wood) check out the incredible night sky. All of this and it's free, on a first-come, first-serve basis.

July is the best time for butterflies and wildflowers. August and early September are the best times to camp when the weather is more consistent and the skeeters are done. It's only 0.3 miles to the Mt. Ashland Ski Area parking lot.

Mt. Ashland Campground provides easy access to the high Siskiyous.

Region 1 — Jacksonville to Emigrant Lake

A picnic table marks a campsite with incredible views at Mt. Ashland campground.

Mt. Ashland Ski Area: The #20 Road turns into County Road #1151 at the ski area's parking lot. The intersection with Old Highway 99 lies 9 miles ahead.

After driving 25 miles or so of beautiful backroads, we are unceremoniously delivered to a paved parking lot, part of the Mount Ashland Ski Area. This asphalt acreage is the beginning of Jackson County Road #1151.

The ski area covers a few hundred acres and is served by four chairlifts. The sometimes fickle snow has been a challenge for the resort in the past. Mother Nature has been mostly generous in some recent years dumping hundreds of inches of snow on Mt. Ashland and the high Siskiyous. About 300 inches of snow is expected to fall in an average 12-month period. Head east past the ski resort buildings and continue downhill on County Road #1151.

County Road #1151 to Old Highway 99: We turn left (north) and head downhill after reaching the Old Highway 99 intersection.

Oregon Backroads Guide to the Pacific Crest Trail

MAP R1.5: MT. ASHLAND TO HIGHWAY 66

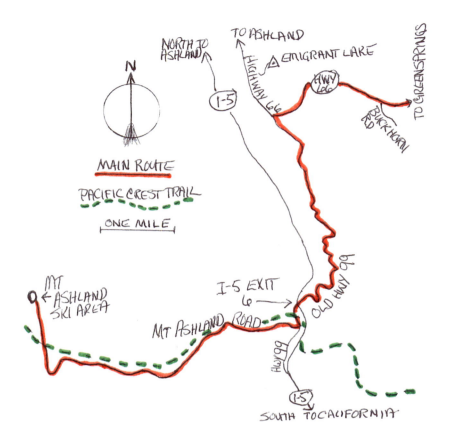

After leaving the ski area, the paved road heads steadily down the mountain with more inspiring views to the south. At **2.0 miles from the ski area we cross the PCT**, elevation 5,987 ft.

On the way downhill look for a few nice turnoffs where you can admire the scenery close up. Some of the road-cuts along the way expose the ancient rocks of Mt. Ashland, a complex geologic formation that started to scrape up (accrete) against the North American Plate on the order of 140 million years ago. In just less than 8 miles we pass the Colestin Valley Road on our right.

Continuing downhill and to the left on the #1151 Road, we come to a stop sign and the intersection of Old Highway 99,

Region 1 — Jacksonville to Emigrant Lake

Look for turnouts where beautiful scenery and the complex geology of Mt. Ashland are on display.

nine miles from Mt. Ashland Ski Area. The Main Route turns left and heads downhill.

To our right and heading south (uphill), Old Highway 99 tops the crest of the Siskiyous and heads into California.

Before the construction of Interstate 5 (the local portion of the interstate was built in 1963–64), this was the main north-south Pacific Highway. Large sections of Old Highway 99 were constructed on the existing wagon road that connected Yreka, California to southern Oregon and points north. Undoubtedly Native Americans used this same, natural way through the Siskiyous for thousands of years before that.

OLD HWY. 99 & COUNTY RD. #1151 INTERSECTION:

Elevation 4,351 ft.

The Main Route turns left and heads downhill on Old Highway 99 northbound, coming to a stop sign adjacent to the freeway in 0.6 miles. We **cross the Pacific Crest Trail** before reaching the I-5 interchange at Exit 6, which is about 10 minutes from

Ashland via the Interstate. **Turn right and go under the freeway** following the signs towards Old 99 and **Highway 66**.

Old Highway 99 to Highway 66: After going under the freeway and immediately to our left is

Callahan's Lodge:
Phone 541-482-1299 • callahanslodge.com

Originally built in 1947 by World War II vet Don Callahan, and subsequently demolished for the construction of I-5, the lodge was reconstructed at its present site in 1965. Sold in 1996 and expanded by the new owners, the lodge was leveled by fire in 2006. Reborn from the ashes is today's Callahan's Lodge. With a fine dining restaurant, banquet facilities, and nineteen luxury rooms, the lodge also has an area for hikers on the PCT to camp, shower, and cache food and supplies for their journey.

Continuing north on Old Highway 99 past Callahan's, the highway winds its way down the northern slope of the Siskiyou Range. Imagine cruising Highway 99 in its heyday,

Even though its name is Irish, Callahan's Lodge is known for Italian food.

Region 1 — Jacksonville to Emigrant Lake

Ashland Mountain House is the oldest surviving structure in southern Oregon.

perhaps on a fine summer afternoon with the top down on your brand new '57 Chevy Belair…woo hoo!

Just before we encounter Highway 66 and the end of Region One we find…

The Ashland Mountain House:
Phone 541-482-2744 • ashlandmountainhouse.com

Rich with history, this is the oldest (documented) surviving structure in southern Oregon. The Ashland Mountain House was originally built as an inn in 1852. At that time it was situated at the crossroads of the **Siskiyou Pass Trail** and the **Applegate Trail**. It became the stage stop when a wagon road was constructed across the Siskiyous and eventually became the residence of the Barron family who grew their land holdings to over 8,000 acres by the turn of the century.

Changing hands in 1960, the buildings were allowed to deteriorate, becoming virtual (junk filled) ruins by the time it was sold again in 2002. Lovingly and completely restored by the new owners over a period of 2 years, this B&B is now one of the premier such establishments in Oregon and deservedly on the National Historic Registry.

Just beyond the Ashland Mountain House we arrive at **Oregon State Highway 66** and the end of Region One. Turn left (head west) to drive to **Emigrant Lake Park**, the town of **Ashland**, and the beginning of Region Two.

END OF REGION ONE

In Region One we explored the National Landmark town of Jacksonville, toured the Upper Applegate Valley, traversed the crest of the Siskiyou Mountains and descended along Old Highway 99 to Emigrant Lake and the town of Ashland. Please watch your step as you exit the bus…The bus for Region Two leaves shortly.

Along the way in Region Two, we will search for more opportunities to unfold the chairs and break out the binoculars. Of course, in keeping with the spirit of the Guide we'll have an eye out for wildlife, play in and on the water, and seek out those places that serve the best food and the coldest beer.

Optional roads allow more points of access to the Pacific Crest Trail while the Main Route heads north along the Cascade Crest from Green Springs Inn, passes by four major lakes, and crosses one of the least traveled passes in the southern Oregon Cascades. Lake of the Woods, Upper Klamath Lake, and Rocky Point are worthwhile places to take extra time to enjoy the scenery and view the bird life. We'll cross open rangeland before arriving at the town of Fort Klamath.

Be forewarned that gas stations are rather rare in the Upper Klamath Basin.

Region Two
Ashland to Fort Klamath

Springtime on Seven Mile Creek in the Upper Klamath Basin with 8,934 ft. Mount Scott in the background.

"Our Journey, whatever the outcome,
provides its own reward."
— *Lawrence M. Krause, Cosmologist*
A Universe from Nothing

The quaint town of Ashland is the starting point for Region Two.
Lithia Park, named after its piped-in mineral water containing
high levels of lithium, incorporates many native plants.

Region 2 — Ashland to Fort Klamath

ROUTE DESCRIPTION

This leg of our journey **begins at I-5, Exit 14 in Ashland**, goes past five major lakes, and ends at the town of Fort Klamath, Oregon. Total distance is about 85 miles.

⇨ **Allow (with some stops) about 5 to 6 hours.**
⇨ **Ashland is the last reliable place for fuel.**

From I-5, Exit 14, Oregon Highway 66 heads east to the crest of the Cascades. Turning north from Highway 66 at Green Springs Inn, the route follows the Cascade Mountains past Hyatt and Howard Prairie Lakes. After crossing 5,730-ft. Griffin Pass, we drive northeast past Lake of the Woods and Upper Klamath Lake. Region Two **ends at the town of Fort Klamath**.

ROAD CONDITIONS

This route is mostly paved with short stretches of improved gravel, suitable for any vehicle. There are no clearance or traction issues in good weather.

Because of the rolling nature of the southern Oregon Cascades, elevations can be deceiving. This route crosses **Griffin Pass, elevation 5,730 ft.**, an unplowed road and among the higher passes in the Oregon Cascades. This pass and the approach roads leading to it are typically closed because of snow during the winter and into the late spring and sometimes until early summer.

Other state highways and most paved county roads along this route are regularly plowed during the winter but may close during heavy snow events. Remember to take the season into account when planning a trip to the high country and go prepared.

MAPS FOR THIS AREA

Listed below are the maps recommended for Region Two.

The *Rogue River National Forest Visitors Map* is available at the Rogue-Siskiyou National Forest Office on Biddle Road near the airport in Medford, Oregon. Call them at 541-618-2200 for National Forest and regional road information. The

Oregon Backroads Guide to the Pacific Crest Trail

Rogue River Forest map overlaps the Winema National Forest roads that are part of Region Two. Updated versions may be available soon. Order U.S. Forest Service maps on-line at fs.usda.gov/rogue-siskiyou.

The Cascade-Siskiyou National Monument and the Soda Mountain Wilderness area are administered by the Bureau of Land Management (BLM). Contact them at 541-618-2200 or look on-line for more information at blm.gov/or/resources.

Find Benchmark Maps at your local sporting goods retailer or on-line at benchmarkmaps.com.

- Rogue River National Forest Visitors Map
- Benchmark Maps – *Oregon Road and Recreation Atlas* – Pages 85, 96, and 97.

Looking west from Rocky Point, Mt. McLoughlin shows its heavily eroded northeast side.

Region 2 — Ashland to Fort Klamath

MAIN ROADS IN ORDER OF TRAVEL

All regional Routes are listed South to North.

Oregon Hwy. 66	The paved road to Green Springs Inn and Hyatt Prairie Rd.
Hyatt Prairie Rd.	The paved road past Hyatt Lake to Howard Prairie Dam Rd.
Howard Prairie Dam Rd.	A dam fine road…hooks up with the Keno Access Rd.
Keno Access Rd.	Access to Keno was obviously a priority in the near past; connects with FS Rd. #2520.
Forest Service Rd. #2520	The improved gravel Griffin Pass Rd., takes us to…
Dead Indian Memorial Rd.	Not sure…But I think it's meant in a positive way. Paved road connects to Lake of the Woods Resort Rd.
Lake of the Woods Resort Rd.	Our connection to Hwy. 140.
Hwy. 140	The state highway connection to Rocky Point Rd.
Rocky Point Rd.	This paved road turns into improved gravel.
Westside Rd.	Past Rocky Point this paved road takes us to the #3100 Rd.
Forest Service Rd. #3100	This dirt road takes us past beaver ponds and riparian areas.
Nicholson Rd.	The paved road to the town of Fort Klamath.

OPTIONAL & SECONDARY ROADS

Buckhorn Rd.	The gravel road option to Hwy 66.
Old Hyatt Prairie Rd.	Gravel road connects Hwy. 66 with Hyatt Prairie Rd.

MAP R2.1: MAIN ROUTE

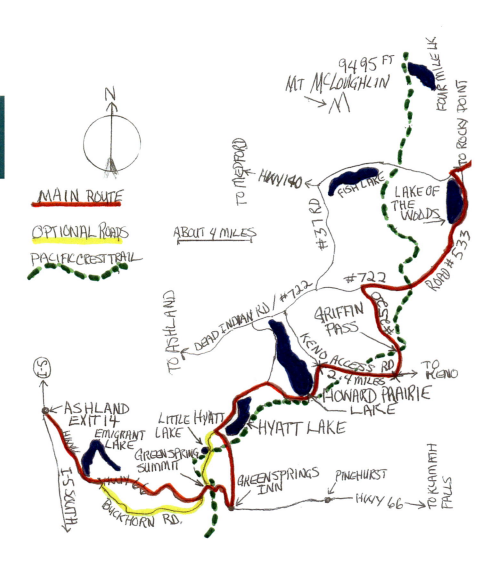

Region 2 — Ashland to Fort Klamath

ROAD NOTES — REGION TWO

This route begins in Ashland at the intersection of Siskiyou Boulevard and I-5, Exit 14, (the south Ashland exit). We head southeast on Oregon Highway 66 from there.

ASHLAND: Elevation 1,895 ft.

Ashland has my vote as the best Oregon town along the I-5 corridor. Sure, Eugene has the award for funky weirdness (to my friends in Eugene, I mean that in the best of ways), and Portland gets the prize for big city soul and bohemian ambience.

Ashland's happy mix of laid-back hippy cool and artistic sophistication makes it the hands-down winner. If you toss in beautiful surroundings (nestled between the Siskiyou and Cascade Mountains), and a generally sunny climate, it's really not even a close contest.

Wander around the side streets and discover trendy restaurants and other flavorful businesses. With a cozy bar and a friendly crew, **Louie's Bar and Grill**, located downtown on the Plaza, offers good food and an impressive menu of reasonably priced

The cozy environs of Louie's Bar and Grill on the Plaza.

dishes. Sample Louie's version of meat on a stick, "coconut chicken skewers," served with a spicy peanut sauce.

Standing Stone Brewing Company, 101 Oak St., prides itself on being a green business using innovative materials and systems in its construction and operation. Try their brick oven baked "pizza rustica" and a cool pint of hand-crafted ale.

The **Oregon Shakespeare Festival** is an important player in the Ashland scene (yes, puns fully intended), as are several other theaters that stage live performances in Ashland and surrounding communities throughout the year. Get more info on-line at osfashland.org

Southern Oregon University is an integral part of the fabric of Ashland. Boasting over 6,500 students, the school's presence brings a younger vibe to downtown.

Downtown Ashland is centered on what locals call **"The Plaza."** Surrounded by several blocks of interesting shops and restaurants, this is the gateway to Lithia Park.

Standing Stone Brewing Company offers good food and great beer.

Region 2 — Ashland to Fort Klamath

Ashland's Plaza is where Lithia Park and the commercial district meet.

Lithia Park: With the Tudor-style buildings of the Oregon Shakespeare Theaters looming above the entrance, the park follows **Ashland Creek** uphill and stretches over 93 acres to the west of town (about 1.4 miles) enticing the stroller with trails, duck ponds, and an ice skating rink in the winter. The park is linear in nature with informative plaques (including the many signs reminding everyone Not! to feed the ducks) describing the history of the park along with botanical and common names of the diverse plantings of trees and shrubs inhabiting the riparian area of the creek.

Interspersed with the playground equipment are eclectic garden sculptures. Volleyball and tennis courts are present for the athletically inclined. In the company of our (sometimes odd) fellow men and women, the park offers many opportunities to linger and enjoy the sound of falling water and experience nature in a near natural environment. Trails connecting uphill from the park lead to the Ashland Watershed and a connection with the **Pacific Crest Trail**.

Oregon Backroads Guide to the Pacific Crest Trail

The water slide at Emigrant Lake Park.

Ashland to Green Springs Inn via Highway 66:

From Exit 14 in south Ashland we head east on Oregon Highway 66. It's 16.7 miles to Green Springs Inn and the turnoff to Hyatt Prairie Road.

At 0.5 miles from town we pass the intersection of Dead Indian Memorial Road on our left. We'll encounter this road again later in our journey.

Still heading east on Highway 66, we encounter Emigrant Lake Park Road at 3.1 miles from Exit 14.

EMIGRANT LAKE PARK: Elevation 2,241 ft.

The park consists of two separate camp areas; one for RVs (32 sites) and the other for car and tent campers (42 sites). Large day-use shelters can be rented for group events. Food concessions and showers are available near the 280-foot water slide, which is operated seasonally. While not a heart stopper, the slide is good wet fun on a hot day.

Emigrant Lake is open for fishing year-round with at least one of the area's two boat launches open in the winter. The fish

Region 2 — Ashland to Fort Klamath

MAP R2.2: EMIGRANT LAKE TO HYATT LAKE

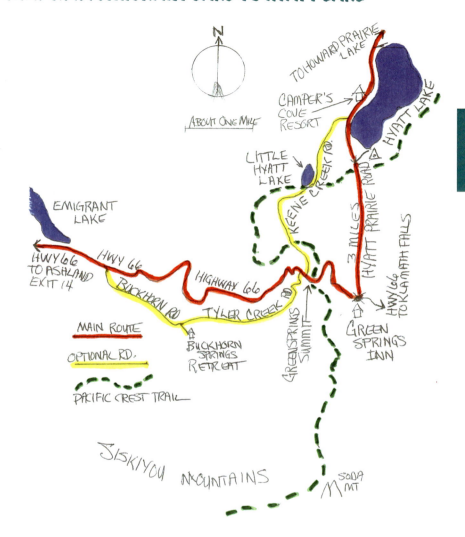

in the lake run the gamut from several warm water species to trout. Check your local regulations before fishing.

Just before entering the park, rounding the curve to our left, is an interesting example of what's known to geologists as the **Hornbook Formation**. A late Cretaceous marine deposit, this unassuming band of fist-sized and smaller cobblestones embedded in the road-cut were formed when this was oceanfront property. No gently sloping sandy beach here, the cobbles are evidence of a wave-tossed shoreline.

Leaving Emigrant Lake Park we **continue east on Highway 66** and intersect Old Highway 99 (the end of Region One) 5.0 miles from Exit 14, elevation 2,285 ft.

Continuing a few miles east on Highway 66 the road grade is mostly flat, so watch out for cyclists.

At 7.7 miles from Exit 14, we encounter the Optional Buckhorn Road on our right.

> ⇨ **Special Note:** *For those who choose not to take the optional Buckhorn Road, the* Main Route *(marked in red on the Guide map) continues below at:* **"Still heading east on Highway 66."**

OPTIONAL BUCKHORN ROAD: Elevation 2,319 ft.

This optional road is marked in yellow on the Guide map. Buckhorn and Tyler Creek Roads are improved gravel, OK for passenger cars.

This optional road heads in the same direction as Highway 66 but stays at lower elevations before climbing steeply and re-joining Highway 66 just west of Green Springs Summit. There are other roads leading off this one that get you closer to trailheads that lead into the Soda Mountain Wilderness. This was the original route of the Applegate Trail and winds past ranch and farm operations as it makes its way towards the Cascade Crest. Madrone stands mixed with pine and conifers line the creek drainage. Watch for wild turkeys along the way.

This road heads southeast along Emigrant Creek before heading east along Tyler Creek Road. Two miles from Highway 66 we come to a "Y" in the road. Tyler Creek Road is to our left, heads uphill, and leads us back to Highway 66. The road to our right leads to a gated turnaround and the entrance to Buckhorn Springs Retreat.

Buckhorn Springs Retreat Center:
2200 Buckhorn Springs Road • 541-488-2200

Region 2 – Ashland to Fort Klamath

Buckhorn Springs Retreat is the site of an historic mineral spring reknowned for its healing properties.

The Center features several cabins for rent and the chance to experience the potential healing properties of the local CO_2 springs. These springs are reputed to be the sacred springs of the Native Americans who inhabited this area for thousands of years, with stories of on-site medicine men who administered the proper "prescriptions" of vapors for the gravely ill. Warring tribes declared a temporary truce for those who could reach the springs. Legend tells us that those who led virtuous lives in the eyes of the Great Spirit would be healed, while those that were lacking would face a less rosy future. Learn more about this enigmatic place at buckhornsprings.org.

From the Tyler Creek intersection it's four miles to Highway 66. We ascend the valley through beautiful open woodlands towards Hobart Bluff.

At 2.5 miles from the Tyler Creek intersection we arrive at Baldy Creek Road (#40-3e-5.0). Keeping to the left we continue uphill. As we near Highway 66 the views get better; Pilot Rock is in clear view to the southwest.

On the edge of the Soda Mountain Wilderness, Pilot Rock has guided travelers for millennia.

Turn right on Highway 66 (uphill) and arrive at Green Springs Summit in less than 0.5 mile. (See **Green Springs Summit Intersection** described below).

Still Heading East on Highway 66: For those not taking "Optional Buckhorn Springs Road," Highway 66 is narrow in places with few opportunities to pull off as we head uphill. The scenery gets better as we come to a pair of small turnouts on the right, 12.0 miles from I-5, Exit 14, elevation 3,651 ft.

Stop and admire the southern view of **Pilot Rock**, elevation 5,909 ft., the core of an old volcano. Pilot Rock has been an iconic landmark for travelers through this region for thousands of years, marking one of the low spot, east-west routes through the Southern Cascades along with the north-south way through the Siskiyous.

On the uphill side of the Highway 66 road-cut, check out the layered, twisted rock exposed here and further up the mountain, evidence of the titanic forces that shaped these mountains.

Region 2 — Ashland to Fort Klamath

Looking east from here we see the Cascade Crest (Hobart Ridge) approaching and at 14.8 miles from Ashland we intersect Soda Mountain Road on our right as we arrive at **Green Springs Summit**.

GREEN SPRINGS SUMMIT INTERSECTION:
Elevation 4,551 ft. The PCT crosses here.

> ⇨ **Important Note:** *Green Springs Inn* and the continuation of the Main Route (marked in red on the Guide map) is 1.3 miles further east of here on Highway 66.
>
> The optional (marked in yellow) Old Hyatt Prairie Road heads north from Green Springs Summit. Travelers who choose to stay on the Main Route, continue below at: *"For those who are still on Highway 66."*

Optional Old Hyatt Prairie Road: This improved gravel road heads north from Green Springs Summit and **crosses the Pacific Crest Trail in 1.1 miles**. We pass a few incongruous mini-mansions along this road before encountering Little Hyatt Lake, 2.7 miles from Green Springs Summit.

The PCT crosses Keene Creek below Little Hyatt dam.

LITTLE HYATT LAKE: Elevation 4,621 ft. No Facilities.

A small dam forms this lake. The PCT trail passes on the south side of the lake and the short hike over the footbridge to the west side of Little Hyatt offers unimproved campsites for walk-ins on BLM land. On the road past the dam, at a small turn-out to the left is a good place to throw a stick for the dog, go swimming, or just relax and watch the fish ringing the surface.

Leaving Little Hyatt Lake, we continue north on Old Hyatt Prairie Road. At 3.5 miles from Green Springs Summit we come to a fork in the road where we'll stay right. At 4.1 miles we come to (new) Hyatt Prairie Road and rejoin the Main Route.

Hyatt Lake lies before us. Turn left to go to **Camper's Cove Resort**, or right towards **Hyatt Lake Campground** (both described below).

For Those Who Are Still on Highway 66: After leaving Green Springs Summit, Highway 66 (the Main Route) winds downhill past Keene Creek Reservoir, 15.3 miles from Ashland and at 16.7 miles we encounter our next wayside.

Green Springs Inn and Hyatt Prairie Road Intersection:
From Green Springs Inn we **head 3.0 miles north on Hyatt Prairie Road to Hyatt Lake Intersection**. The Cascade-Siskiyou National Monument Information Center is also located at this intersection.

The Green Springs Inn
Elevation 4,559 ft. • 541-890-6435

There's more to the Green Springs Inn than meets the eye. The restaurant features great steaks, homemade soups, salads, and breads. They also serve a hearty breakfast and lunch with juicy burgers and fries. Good food seems to be their goal.

A small selection of camper's items and a nice selection of beers are on tap and in the cooler are available. Live music on the weekends and a summer mountain music festival add to the smile on your face and feel of the Green Springs Inn. The country surrounding the Inn is ground zero for the Cascade-Siskiyou National Monument. The proximity of the new

Region 2 — Ashland to Fort Klamath

Great food and luxury cabins await the traveler at Green Springs Inn.

Soda Mountain Wilderness, combined with the many other recreational opportunities in the area, puts the Inn at the center of many new four-season activities. The Inn also offers a free beer to all thru-hikers on the PCT.

A surprising number of people (considering the elevation) live year-round in the immediate area, and the Inn serves as the hub of the Green Springs community, functioning as the local meeting place for good food, conversation, and toe tappin.'

The Inn also rents five beautiful, privately situated cabins overlooking Keene Creek. Each stoutly constructed (there is a sawmill and a solar-heated lumber kiln on the property) and nicely appointed structure sits on its own lot and features a hot tub or custom tiled shower. The owners (the McGuire family) are at work completing five more cabins (as of March 2013) situated on a sunny southwest knoll of their 150-acre property.

Along with luxurious cabins, the Inn offers lodging in an eight-room motel for summer travelers. Cross country skiers and snowmobilers headquarter here in the winter.

THE CASCADE-SISKIYOU NATIONAL MONUMENT

This area was chosen as the first National Monument to preserve biological diversity rather than designated for its scenic or geological attractions.

Influence from the Cascades, Klamath-Siskiyou Mountains, and the Great Basin habitats have shaped the local plants and animals here. Largely spared the heavy glaciations of the last Ice Age (which ended about 11,500 years ago) this crossroads of northern California, southern Oregon, and the Great Basin hosts an amazing diversity of life. The **Soda Mountain Wilderness** lies just south of the Green Springs Inn.

Green Springs Inn to Hyatt Lake: We leave Highway 66 and drive 3.0 miles north to Hyatt Lake Intersection. Directly across Highway 66 from Green Springs Inn is the beginning of the Hyatt Prairie Road. To the east of Hyatt Prairie Road is Chinquapin Mountain, elevation 6,134 ft.

The **chinquapin tree** (or "giant" chinquapin) is a northwest native and related to the chestnut. This hardwood tree is evergreen and generally occurs on the north side of slopes. Its spiny, coated seed pods with tiny edible nuts (not worth the trouble) help identify this tree.

HYATT LAKE INTERSECTION: Elevation 5,000 ft.

From here we turn left and head north on Hyatt Prairie Road. It's 2.0 miles to Campers Cove Resort and 5.6 miles to our turnoff on Howard Prairie Dam Road.

For those purists and map readers, there appears to be a road that goes through on the east side of Hyatt Lake (East Hyatt Lake Road) that more closely follows the PCT. This road has been gated for years but the mapmakers haven't caught up yet.

But wait! There's a nice BLM campground on the east side called (oddly enough) **Hyatt Lake Campground**. Less than a block ahead, the campground features 2 boat ramps, 47 pull-through camps and 7 walk-in sites. Look for some fun playground equipment adjacent to the day-use area.

Just past Hyatt Lake Campground, **Wildcat Campground** is smaller and located on a peninsula. The road ends at a gate shortly after the entrance to Wildcat Camp. There's a pleasant campsite for PCT hikers in the woods to the east.

Because this road is gated, there are some places to park along this quiet-side that give you the opportunity to walk through some relatively undisturbed high country wetlands and meadows. This can also be a good place to cross-country ski or snowshoe in the wintertime. Look for osprey nests and diving cormorants along the shoreline in the spring, summer, and fall.

Heading north on Hyatt Lake Prairie Road, it's two miles to Camper's Cove Resort.

Camper's Cove Resort:
hyattlake.com • 541-482-3331 • 7900 Hyatt Prairie Road

The resort has a café (with an extensive menu and pretty darn good food) and a small store. Cabins are for rent year-round. During the summer season kayak and canoe rentals are available. Camping, fishing, bird watching, and boating

A snowy morning in March at Hyatt Lake.

are the pastimes here in the summer time. Snowmobiling and cross country skiing are popular in the winter months.

Fishing for (mostly small) bass in the lake can be productive. Some occasional lunker bass weighing over 5 lbs. are hooked here. Every year a few rainbow trout (big enough to eat the many smaller bass) measuring well over 20 inches are caught here. Perch fishing can be fun for kids from the shore. Try a piece of worm three feet under a bobber.

Continuing less than 0.5 miles north on Hyatt Lake Prairie Road, we come to the Osprey Viewing Area with a lakeside bench and informational signs describing the typical birds that may be seen from here. From the viewing area it's 3.8 miles to Howard Prairie Dam Road.

⇨ **Special Note:** *Howard Prairie Recreation Area and the adjacent Howard Prairie Resort and Marina lie 1.5 miles north of here along the Hyatt Prairie Road. See below for the* **"Howard Prairie Dam Road Intersection"** *description and the continuation of the* Main Route.

Hyatt Lake Resort has a restaurant and rents cabins year-round.

Region 2 — Ashland to Fort Klamath

HOWARD PRAIRIE LAKE RECREATION AREA:
Elevation 4,526 ft.

Howard Prairie Resort operates a small store along with a café and marina. A rock jetty extends into the lake providing shelter for the marina and handicap accessible fishing. The Resort rents deluxe RV trailers with hook-ups, boats, kayaks, and canoes. RV, tent, and car camping are available in the adjacent campground. Gasoline is available here for cars and boats.

American white pelicans with wingspans generally over 100 inches are easy to spot; these birds are not uncommon on area lakes. **Sandhill cranes** are sometimes seen in the marshes and open woodlands at this elevation. Often heard before

MAP R2.3: HYATT LAKE TO PEDERSON SNO-PARK

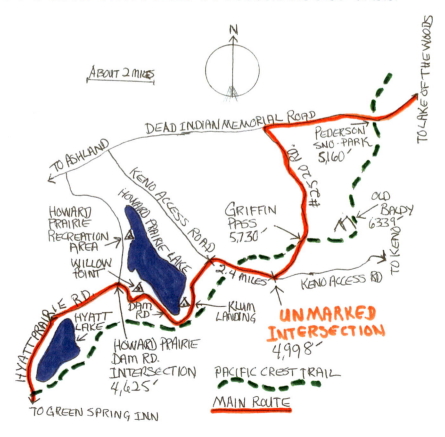

seen, the three-foot tall adults are sometimes easy to find if approached slowly during the mating season (April and May) and are further identified by their red crests.

HOWARD PRAIRIE DAM ROAD INTERSECTION:
Elevation 4,625 ft.

The Main Route turns right and heads northeast on Howard Prairie Dam Road. From this intersection it's 3.8 miles to Keno Access Road.

In just 0.6 miles we find Willow Point on our left. **Willow Point Campground**, located at the south end of the lake, features a boat ramp and a hikers trail (about 0.3 miles) to the Red Rocks, a popular place for walk-in bank fishing. At 2.5 miles past Willow Point we come to Klum Landing on our left. **Klum Landing Campground**, located on the east side of the lake has a boat launch, camping, day-use area, and showers.

Leaving Klum Landing, keep an eye to your left for an unmarked dirt road. This road goes to an informal viewpoint and rocky beach adjacent to the dam, a nice spot for a picnic or to let the

Howard Prairie Resort's store, cafe, and marina offer boat rentals, campsites, RV rentals, and gasoline.

Region 2 — Ashland to Fort Klamath

Willow Point Campground has a great boat ramp, shown here in winter, high and dry.

dog go swimming. There's a small (no fee) slide-in boat launch here for canoes and smaller boats but no camping.

Back on the main road there's a dip as the road passes over the irrigation canal. Before we reach Keno Access Road, a couple of dirt tracks (not for passenger cars) head west towards the lake and a few informal campsites on the shoreline.

Still heading northeast on the Dam Road (it's really not that bad!) we soon arrive at the **Keno Access Road intersection**.

⇨ **Special Note:** *Anyone who writes a good travel guide has obviously spent a great deal of time exploring the areas they describe. Discovering secret places is part of the job description…so, with some trepidation (since I once hauled a pick-up load of trash out of there), I share with my readers the Secret Swimming Hole at the Old Quarry.* **Please note that clothing is optional.**

Instead of turning right (the Main Route) on the Keno Access Road, turn left and head west. I'll leave it up to you to discover exactly where the quarry is (about 3.7 miles) but look for layered rocks along the roadside adjacent to an unmarked road to your left. Shhh! Don't tell anyone…Please pick up your trash.

KENO ACCESS ROAD INTERSECTION:
Elevation 4,622 ft.

⇨ **Special Note!** *Our next turnoff is on an* **UNMARKED** *road. Check your odometer and* **drive exactly 2.4 miles** *east on the Keno Access Road to the Griffin Pass Road. Consult the Guide map.*

Heading East on the Keno Access Road: In 0.9 miles we encounter the crossing of the **Pacific Crest Trail** and 0.4 miles past that we see the #38-4E-34 Road on our left. In another 1.1 miles we come to an unmarked road to our left, a total of 2.4 miles from the Dam Road Intersection. This is the Griffin Pass Road, also designated as the #2520 Road.

#2520 ROAD INTERSECTION: Elevation 4,998 ft.
⇨ **This road is not signed.**

From the Keno Access Road we'll turn left and head north across Griffin Pass. It's a total of 5.3 miles from this intersection to our next turnoff at Dead Indian Memorial Road.

Remnants of pavement persist for the first mile of this road before turning to improved gravel. The road heads steeply up through scattered woodlands with some washboards but is suitable for any vehicle. Continuing 1.7 miles from Keno Access Road, we reach **Griffin Pass** and the intersection of the **Pacific Crest Trail**.

GRIFFIN PASS AREA: Elevation 5,730 ft.

This pass (among the higher passes in the Oregon Cascades) divides BLM land to the south from National Forest land to the north. The drier southern slope is open grassland with scattered second- and third-growth timber. Big trees on the north side of the pass, marked by a cattle guard, delineate the National Forest boundary.

Big Spring (about 150 yards south of the summit) provides an easy water supply for PCT hikers passing through here. Flowing from a pipe, the cold, clear water (not tested for

Region 2 — Ashland to Fort Klamath

drinking quality) is a refreshing treat on a hot day. Adjacent to the spring is a single walk-in campsite tucked into the trees. The surrounding area is a good place in the fall to hunt for chanterelles and other edible mushrooms.

Sugar pine (*Pinus lambertiana*), the tallest and largest of all pines, occurs in the Oregon Cascades south of Santiam Pass. Look on the ground along the Griffin Pass Road for the giant size (10–12 inches) pine cones that distinguish this long-lived tree from the other pines. These giant pine cones can weigh 3 or 4 pounds when they're green and hang above the ground 150 feet or more. It's wise to pay attention when squirrels are harvesting these cones. The sweet sap of these trees was considered a delicacy by Native Americans but can be laxative when consumed in any quantity.

Heading north from Griffin Pass, we drive through beautiful stands of big firs and pines, crossing Big Draw Creek as we head downhill (watch out for the dips in the road) and meet up with Dead Indian Memorial Road.

Near Griffin Pass, the cowdog guards the giant cones from further squirrel predation.

Oregon Backroads Guide to the Pacific Crest Trail

MAP R2.4: LAKE OF THE WOODS TO FORT KLAMATH

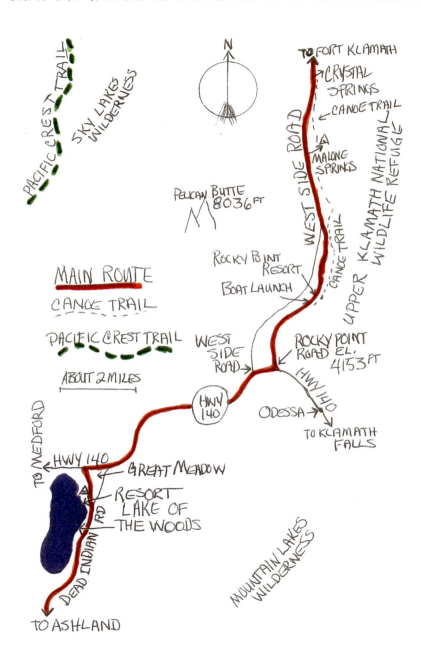

Region 2 — Ashland to Fort Klamath

DEAD INDIAN MEMORIAL ROAD: Elevation 4,814 ft.

The Main Route turns right and heads east on Dead Indian Memorial Road. It's 11.2 miles to our next turnoff at Lake of the Woods Resort, Road #3750.

At 3.4 miles from the Griffin Pass Road, we encounter the Pederson Sno-Park and the intersection of the Pacific Crest Trail. It's here we cross over into Klamath County and enter the Winema National Forest.

BROWN MOUNTAIN: Peak elevation 7,340 ft.

This is the dominant geographical feature as we head northeast from Griffin Pass towards Lake of the Woods. Brown Mountain is a serious volcano in its own right. While not as impressive visually as its 9,495-ft. counterpart to the north (Mt. McLoughlin), Brown Mountain and associated vents have produced some impressive amounts of lava (as tall as a 25-story building in places).

The mountain is actually just a cinder cone perched atop the larger shield volcano (as opposed to a steep-sided

The view of Brown Mountain from Lake of the Woods boat ramp.

stratovolcano like Mt. McLoughlin) overlying many square miles of volcanic activity. Looking in places like the magma just cooled off last week, the lava fields present a natural barrier to travelers heading north along the Cascade Crest. The PCT crosses large sections of vulcan landscape as it heads north towards its rendezvous with the Sky Lakes Wilderness.

Fortunately for us this eruption is older than it looks, occurring thousands of years ago, (the last eruptions appear to be about 2,000 years old)…and road builders have been busy working their way around it.

An excellent place to view Brown Mountain is from the boat ramp at Lake of the Woods Resort.

Lake of the Woods Resort Road #3750: It's a short drive to the resort's driveway so keep a sharp eye to the left. From the resort entrance to the intersection of Highway 140 it's one mile.

LAKE OF THE WOODS AREA:
Elevation 4,949 ft. at the lake

Located in a deep chasm between lava-cloaked Brown Mountain to the west and the 7,700-foot-plus peaks of the Mountain Lakes Wilderness to the east, Lake of the Woods covers 1,146 surface acres and supports a healthy fishery. It's also one of the most popular places to recreate in southern Oregon. On hot summer weekends, the water skiers and jet skis take over the lake in the afternoons.

Fishing for rainbow trout and kokanee is the main pastime here for fishermen (and fisherwomen too). Some impressive brown trout inhabit these waters and Lake of the Woods is one of the few lakes in Oregon open to night fishing. Many cabins and year round residences dot the shoreline but since this is National Forest land, the entire shoreline is open to bank angling. Check local regulations before fishing.

Camping is available at the resort and two other popular campgrounds on the lake.

Region 2 — Ashland to Fort Klamath

Some walk-in campsites at Aspen Point are waterfront.

Sunset Campground: Located about midway along the east side of the almost four-mile-long lake, this is where the summer time action is. This huge (and heavily used) campground and day-use area is within walking distance (about a mile) of the Resort and the Rainbow Bay picnic area. Sunset Campground also features a boat ramp.

Aspen Point Campground: This extensive campground features a boat ramp and day-use area with a connection to **hiking and mountain biking trails**. The most low-key campground on the lake, Aspen Point features several pull-through sites and many walk-in tent sites closer to the lake. Lake of the Woods Resort is an easy walk from here.

LAKE OF THE WOODS RESORT: Elevation 4,956 ft.

Established in 1922 the sprawling resort consists of the store and marina at the boat ramp, and a separate bar and restaurant, which were updated in 2011. With boat rentals at the marina and live music on an outdoor stage many summer weekends, Lake of the Woods is one of the top destination resorts in

Lake of the Woods Lodge is one of the top destination resorts in southern Oregon.

southern Oregon. The resort rents cabins starting at $129 (two nights minimum) and has 25 RV sites. During the summer months the resort hosts an all-you-can-eat barbeque and live music on their lakefront stage. There's room for dancing next to the stage and a bonfire is lit for after music relaxation.

The bar is cozy (and has the nicest bathrooms in the Southern Cascades) with a great selection of Oregon microbrews on tap. The restaurant serves up hearty food and is open for breakfast, lunch, and dinner during the summer. Auto gas is available at the store and boat fuel is available dockside.

The beloved "Stagecoach Ride," enjoyed by generations of visitors to the resort has been retired (look for a photo on oregonbackroads.com). The new Jet-Ski Ride costs 50 cents and now rides the waves at the entrance to Lake of the Woods Store.

Highway 140: We head east on Highway 140 a distance of 7.2 miles to the Rocky Point Road turnoff.

Region 2 — Ashland to Fort Klamath

The new ride at Lake of the Woods is for children of all ages.

⇨ **Important Note!** *Before reaching the Rocky Point Road, we encounter the major intersection and turnoff to Crater Lake/Fort Klamath on our left (the Westside Road). Don't turn here; proceed another 0.4 miles east on Highway 140 to the signed Rocky Point Road turnoff and the continuation of the* Main Route.

From Lake of the Woods Resort Road we turn right on Highway 140 and head east past the **Great Meadow**. Features like the Great Meadow are somewhat common in the Southern Cascades but few are as big as the Great Meadow. Scooped out originally by ice fields, shallow lakes were formed when the climate warmed. Sediment has helped to fill them in.

In the case of the Great Meadow, drainage ditches were dug in the early 20th century to help the process along (for better or worse). Amenities include a large parking area to accommodate the snow park, restrooms, and an information board with a map.

Oregon Backroads Guide to the Pacific Crest Trail

Before Highway 140 turns sharply north, we pass the intersection of Dead Indian Memorial Road on our right.

Looming directly above of us, as Highway 140 heads north, is **Pelican Butte**, elevation 8,036 ft. From our perspective this shield volcano looks uniform but the northeast side (much like Mt. McLoughlin) has been scooped away by glaciers. This bowl (easily seen from Fort Klamath) is popular with snowmobilers and backcountry skiers.

A ski resort was once proposed for this mountain; money swapped hands and some regulators passed judgment, but nothing has yet happened. Pelican Butte lies well east of the Cascade Crest and despite its "impressive for this neck of the woods" elevation, rarely gets enough regular snow to support a commercial operation. There's a lookout on top with a 360-degree view; are your eyes good enough to spot it from Highway 140?

In 6.8 miles from Lake of the Woods Road we arrive at the intersection of **Westside Road** with a sign indicating Crater

Pelican Butte, elevation 8,036 feet, was once considered for a ski development.

Region 2 — Ashland to Fort Klamath

This native-inspired boat is aground next to the Rocky Point Road.

Lake and Fort Klamath to our left. **Don't turn here**; this is the county highway and has surprisingly little exposure to Upper Klamath Lake.

To get a better look at the lake and the town of Rocky Point, the Main Route **continues east on Highway 140 another 0.4 miles** to the signed turnoff to Rocky Point Road. We'll meet up with the Westside Road again in 5.2 miles.

⇨ **Special Note:** *The tiny burg of Odessa lies about two miles further east on Highway 140 (towards Klamath Falls).* **There's a small store with gas.** *Nearby is a compact Winema Forest campground on Odessa Creek with a steep dirt boat launch. Odessa is the closest place to fuel up (short of driving to the town of Klamath Falls), and for those following this guide through Region Three, the last place to fuel up before Crater Lake National Park.*

Rocky Point Road: We stay on this road for 5.2 miles to its junction with Westside Road. Turning north on Rocky Point Road, we wind past many homes and cabins. This place gets its name from the fact that most of Klamath Lake shorelines are mucky and shallow, making landing a boat or building a structure difficult. Rocky Point rests on a solid shelf of basalt with a fairly deep and sheltered harbor. Before the roads were improved in the area, a regular ferry and mail boat ran from the town of Klamath Falls to Rocky Point and Odessa.

Keep an eye on the right for the native-inspired Klamath boat, aground next to the Rocky Point Road.

On the lake side of the road, look for the **Point Comfort Lodge.**

Point Comfort Lodge
831-475-7306 • 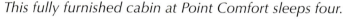pointcomfortlodge.com

Built in 1912 this structure and its furnishings represent the classic "grand" lakefront lodge of the period. The Lodge has seven bedrooms and five baths and a huge, fully equipped kitchen.

Also two very attractive cabins are for rent on the Point Comfort property. The Carriage House comes fully furnished, sleeps three comfortably, and rents from $125 a night with

This fully furnished cabin at Point Comfort sleeps four.

Region 2 — Ashland to Fort Klamath

Looking toward Odessa from the Rocky Point boat launch.

two nights minimum. The more rustic 1940s cabin also is fully furnished and sleeps four, $125 per with two nights minimum. Both cabins have furnished kitchens and provide bed linens.

At 2.5 miles from Highway 140 we arrive at the paved **Rocky Point Boat Launch**. This is the southern end of the **Upper Klamath Lake Canoe Trail** with adequate ramp and docks to accommodate much larger boats. The dock also provides wheelchair accessible fishing.

Launch your canoe here and paddle south about a half-mile along the shore to the mouth of Harriman Creek. Head up the creek (with a paddle) and gaze at the giant trout. Klamath Lake is open year-round, but check the regulations before fishing the tributaries. At the head of the creek, Harriman Springs flows from the rocks.

Rocky Point Resort:
541-356-2287

Located on an arm of Upper Klamath Lake connecting to Crystal Creek, the resort is owned by the Oregon Oddfellows.

The restaurant at Rocky Point Resort offers great views of the lake and wildlife from every table.

Many serious fishermen from around the northwest converge on the lake during May and June in search of rainbow trout up to 15 pounds. No sir, that's not a misprint…15-pound (and no doubt larger) trout swim these waters.

A news item from several years ago recounts the story of a six foot-plus sturgeon hooked and fought in view of witnesses lining the Rocky Point Resort deck. It's not hard to accept these fish tales as true when you look at the thousands of acres of interconnecting lakes, marshes, springs, and rivers making up the Upper Klamath Basin.

The restaurant serves dinner at lakeside with every table a view seat. Pot roast is a favorite among guests. A small store attaches to the office and offers beverages, snack items, and fishing tackle.

The resort rents power boats along with canoes and kayaks during the April 1 through October 31 season. There's boat fuel at the marina.

Trailer sites with power and water are available along with four cabins and five motel rooms. They also have several incredible lakeshore tent sites.

UPPER KLAMATH LAKE

This is the largest freshwater lake by area in Oregon and the largest natural freshwater lake west of the Great Lakes. Popular with bird watchers and fishermen, this wetland along with its connecting rivers grows some big trout (see above). Look for American white pelicans, sandhill cranes, and American avocets in these environs.

Upper Klamath National Wildlife Refuge: Once upon a time the **Klamath Basin** spanned over 180,000 acres of shallow lakes and marshes. Headwaters to the mighty Klamath River, these diverse wetlands attracted prodigious flocks of birds along with fish and amphibians. Native people have inhabited this area for thousands of years harvesting the rich bounty of this generous land.

Plenty of berths are available to dock your boat at Rocky Point Resort.

Today the Klamath Basin is much changed. The Bureau of Reclamation began in 1905 to drain the wetlands and create agricultural and ranch land. Perhaps 25 percent of the originally extensive marshes and shallow lakes remain today.

The U.S. Fish and Wildlife Service in cooperation with the Bureau of Reclamation run the show in the Klamath Basin. These agencies have (unenviably) tried to balance the needs of wildlife and the sometimes competing needs of modern industrial agriculture.

The National Wildlife Refuge is devoted to protecting what's left. The diverse wetlands and forests of the reserve still attract millions of migratory birds yearly. The Klamath Basin National Wildlife Refuge is divided into six individual refuges. The Upper Klamath Refuge extends along the northwest side of Upper Klamath Lake and includes the **Upper Klamath Canoe Trail**.

Upper Klamath Canoe Trail:
The canoe trail leads paddlers through some primal marshland. Bird watching is of course unavoidable. Birdsong and wind through the rushes fill the air most days. Different routes head north to south.

Malone Springs has three campsites and a boat launch.

Region 2 — Ashland to Fort Klamath

The Upper Klamath Canoe Trail is a great way to see birds, Wocus lilies, and the occasional beaver dam up close.

The boat launch at Rocky Point represents the southern end of the water trail and Crystal Springs anchors the northern "trailhead." Malone Springs Campground and boat launch is in the middle.

Road #3525 Intersection with Westside Road: Here we'll turn right and head north on the Westside Road. Its 11.0 miles from here to our turnoff on the #3100 Road. In 0.8 miles we encounter the Malone Springs Road on our right.

Malone Springs: Drive this short road towards the lake and find a small camp area with a boat launch suitable for launching canoes and kayaks. The campsite is unimproved with an outhouse facility. Malone Springs is a popular launch point for day paddles south to Rocky Point. Head north from Malone Springs and paddle to Crystal Springs Lodge.

Back on Westside Road, it's 3.4 miles to Crystal Springs Recreation Site.

Crystal Springs Recreation Site: It's 6.8 miles from here to our turnoff on Forest Service Road #3100.

The very dog-friendly Crystal Woods Lodge is hospitable for your entire entourage, furry faces and all.

Find restrooms here with accessible vault toilets. Originally the site of a school, it's at the northern end of the Upper Klamath Canoe Trail now. This is a popular place for birding and is part of the Klamath Birding Trail. For more information on bird watching opportunities in the Klamath Basin and the Upper Klamath National Wildlife Refuge, look on-line at: klamathbirdingtrail.com. Adjacent to the recreation site is **Crystal Woods Lodge**.

Crystal Woods Lodge:
866-381-2322

For those who choose to travel with a pack of dogs (three or more) you know the look you receive when you check-in to any place of lodging — eyes wide open with a wary look. If you're the proud master of let's say five dogs, you probably need a guide book of your own naming those places that will accept you and your pack…On that short list of accepting places would be the Crystal Woods Lodge.

Perched on the northern end of the canoe trail, the lodge is all about dogs. The owner has raced her dogs in the Iditarod and the seven rooms in the lodge are each named after a way-point on the Alaskan sled dog trail. Every cozy room has its own bath, dog crates, and wool mattress pad. Guests have communal access to a fully furnished commercial kitchen and outdoor grill. The common area is ample and the grounds are expansive with canoes and places for dogs to splash and play just down the hill. Paddling and bird watching are popular activities. Bring your Wi-Fi capable devices if you must...the lodge provides connectivity.

Heading North on the Westside Road:

> ⇨ **Special Note!** *After leaving Crystal Springs, the West-side Road heads straight north for several miles before the road curves sharply east. It's at this curve in the highway we meet the intersection of the #3100 Road.* **If you start heading east on the Seven Mile Road you've gone too far. Refer to Map R3.1.**

Forest Service Road #3100: The gravel #3100 Road heads north along the rocky shelf edging the Upper Klamath Basin. It's basically an unpaved extension of Westside Road. Some

The many springs below the #3100 Road are fascinating.

maps show this byway as the #3300 Road and some show it as the Westside Road; regardless of designation it's a beautiful three-mile drive along the western rim of the Upper Klamath Basin when the weather is dry.

Numerous springs flow eastward just below the roadbed. About a mile from the pavement the views to the east open up. Stop and look for the many springs, large and small that line the hillside below the road. Just past the first springs look for evidence of beaver ponds next to the road on the right.

In 2.8 miles from the Westside Road we encounter an intersection where we **stay right and head east on the #3100 Road**. The road crosses a bridge over beautiful Seven Mile Creek as we leave the Winema National Forest and the #3100 Road becomes the paved Nicholson Road.

Nicholson Road: The Nicholson Road heads straight east through wide-open ranchland for 3.8 miles, taking us to the organically delicious Jo's Motel and the town of Fort Klamath.

END OF REGION TWO

Looking back in Region Two we've traveled across the Cascade Crest from western Oregon and the Siskiyou Mountains to eastern Oregon and the Klamath River drainage. If the weather was clear, we got a good look at the up-start volcanoes of southern Oregon's High Cascades. After passing by the largest lake in Oregon, we arrive at the town of Fort Klamath.

Region Three gives us lots of chances to strap on the hiking boots for short hikes to as many as six waterfalls along the Main Route and optional roads. The high point (literally) of the upcoming region is of course Crater Lake National Park, but don't forget to spend time in the Diamond Lake area too. I highly recommend the optional waterfalls tour on the North Umpqua River, west of Lemolo Lake. It's easy to spend several days (or weeks) in this part of Oregon and just scratch the surface of the scenic and recreational opportunities in Region Three. Enjoy!

Region Three
Fort Klamath to Lemolo Lake

Within Oregon's only National Park, Crater Lake is the deepest lake in the United States with a maximum depth of 1,949 feet.

"Not all those who wander are lost."
— *J.R.R. Tolkien*, **The Fellowship of the Ring**

The lake was formed 7,700 years ago when the volcano, Mount Mazama, collapsed. The caldera rim ranges between 7,000 and 8,000 feet in elevation.

Region 3 — Fort Klamath to Lemolo Lake

ROUTE DESCRIPTION

This part of our journey **begins at the town of Fort Klamath** Oregon, continues around the east side of Crater Lake National Park, past Diamond Lake and **ends at Lemolo Lake**. Total distance is about 70 miles.

> ⇨ **Allow (with several stops) about 6 hours.**

If you choose to do the optional waterfall tour, set aside an additional 2 hours.

ROAD CONDITIONS

The Region Three route is paved and suitable for any vehicle with no clearance or traction issues in good weather. Because of the high elevations (approaching 8,000 ft.) in Crater Lake Park, the North Entrance and the East Rim Road are typically closed because of snow by late October. The East Rim Road is closed no later than November 1st in any event. Road crews usually start plowing the roads with the aim of re-opening in the early summer (in typical snow years).

The road from the Annie Spring (south) Entrance Station to Crater Lake Lodge is plowed and kept open throughout the year but may close periodically during heavy snow events. All other roads described in Region Three are regularly plowed during the winter.

Beware that the Park has begun closing the East Rim Drive to motorized traffic for one weekend in September. In 2013 the road was closed September 21st and 22nd. The West Rim Drive will remain open during this closure.

MAPS FOR THIS AREA

The *Rogue River National Forest Visitors Map* is available at the Rogue-Siskiyou National Forest Office on Biddle Road near the airport in Medford, Oregon. Call them at 541-618-2200 for National Forest and regional road information.

The Rogue River National Forest Map overlaps the Winema National Forest Roads that are part of Region Three. Order National Forest Maps on-line at fs.usda.gov. Look for the

Diamond Lake Ranger District and Umpqua National Forest maps at fs.fed.us/r6/umpqua.

Crater Lake National Park is administered by the National Park Service. Contact park headquarters at 541-594-3000 or look on-line for more information at nps.gov/crla.

Find Benchmark Maps at your local sporting goods retailer or on-line at benchmarkmaps.com.

Listed below are the maps recommended for Region Three:

- Diamond Lake Ranger District Map
- Umpqua National Forest Map
- Rogue River National Forest Visitors Map
- Benchmark Maps: *Oregon Road and Recreation Atlas*, page 85

MAIN ROADS IN ORDER OF TRAVEL

All Regional Routes are listed South to North

Hwy. 62	The paved highway from Fort Klamath to the Park entrance.
National Park Roads	The paved roads connecting with Highway 138.
Hwy. 138	The paved Hwy. to the Hwy. 230 junction.
Hwy. 230	We're on this road for about a city block before our turn to Diamond Lake.
Rd. #6592/ Diamond Lake Area	Hugs the east side of Diamond Lake.
Highway 138	After leaving Diamond Lake we're back on Hwy.138 for 5.7 miles.
Rd. #2610/ Birds Point Rd.	The road to Lemolo Lake Resort and the end of Region 3.

Region 3 — Fort Klamath to Lemolo Lake

MAP R3.1: MAIN ROUTE

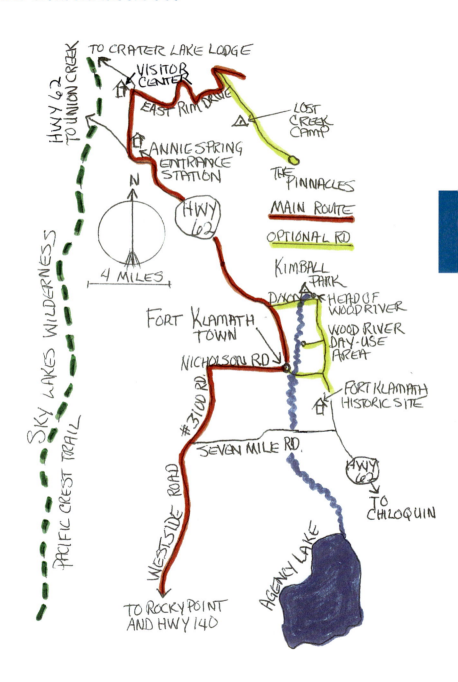

ROAD NOTES — REGION THREE

Starting in Fort Klamath, the following notes give details about the sights, history, and attractions along the way.

FORT KLAMATH TOWN: Elevation 4,175 ft.

From here we drive west on Highway 62 to Crater Lake National Park. To explore the **Optional Wood River Loop** (described below) follow Highway 62 east.

⇨ **Special Note!** *The town of Fort Klamath, located on the beautiful Wood River, is just up the road from the historic army post of the same name.*

This small community is the epitome of rural, east-slope southern Oregon. Open spaces and snow-capped peaks in the distance could be anywhere in the west. Squint your eyes and you could easily be looking at Colorado or Wyoming. Several large ranches dot the well-watered Upper Klamath Basin, raising cattle and sheep. It's easy to estimate that the ruminants far outnumber the humans in this area during the grazing season. Springtime comes late to the basin because of the high elevation but when it shows

"Where's the beef?" Near Fort Klamath in the wide open spaces, few things are sadder than a cow dog without cows.

Region 3 — Fort Klamath to Lemolo Lake

You can get almost anything you want at the deliciously organic Jo's Motel, from lodging to groceries, but no gasoline.

up… it's a glorious time of the year with crystal clear skies, snowy mountains, and knee-high grass rippling in the breeze.

Few commercial establishments are in town; a grocery store stocked with organic goods is located at Jo's Motel. The nearest gasoline is 14 miles east in Chiloquin. Gas is also available in Crater Lake Park during the warmer months. Several lodging options are available. **Sun Pass Ranch** is a bed and breakfast and horse hotel.

Sun Pass Ranch:
541-381-2882

The **Aspen Inn Motel** features two furnished cottages (one with a pool table) for rent along with cabins and motel rooms. The motel is very dog friendly and has a great outdoor area that your furry friends will love.

Aspen Inn:
541-381-2321

Jo's Motel offers lodging, camping, and a menu of organic food items in the deli.

Jo's Motel:
541-381-2234
Try Robin's delicious muffins with a hot espresso. The motel proudly advertises no phones, no TV, and no Wi-Fi. Jo's is also very dog friendly, and pets are welcome for an extra charge. Each neatly kept, cabin-like room has its own kitchen and carport, lending it the nostalgic air of a 1960s era family vacation motel.

⇨ **Special Note:** *To follow the optional Wood River Loop (the yellow route on Map R3.1), cross the Wood River Bridge as you head east out of town on Hwy. 62.*

OPTIONAL WOOD RIVER LOOP:

Historic Fort Klamath: Old Fort Klamath was located near timber and a good source of water, but nowhere near emigrant wagon roads the Army was assigned to protect from Indian attack. This military outpost with sweeping views of the Upper Klamath Basin was occupied until 1889 when it was officially abandoned. The buildings of the fort were crushed by 20 feet of

Little remains of historic Fort Klamath but the graves of the four men executed for their roles in the Modoc Indian Wars.

Region 3 — Fort Klamath to Lemolo Lake

accumulated snow the previous winter, and anything that was left after the military's departure was carted off by local residents. The structures present today are reconstructions; the only historic traces left are the graves of the four native Americans who were executed here for their part in the Modoc Indian War. The museum is open from late May through Labor Day.

Wood River Day Use Area: This pleasant park located on the banks of the Wood River offers wheelchair-accessible boardwalks connecting with wooden benches located strategically on the river's edge. This is a great place to picnic and a good spot for birding along the river and in the many acres of woods along the access road. Several picnic tables are adjacent to the parking area, lined by a stand of quaking aspen. Fly-fishing on the Wood River is a popular (and sometimes very productive) pastime.

Jackson F. Kimball State Park: Marking the **headwaters of the Wood River**, this park offers twelve fee sites with no water and no hook-ups. The mosquitoes can be a problem early in the season. The good news is it's only $5 to camp. Canoeists and kayakers **launch here for floats down the Wood River**.

The Wood River Day Use Area is accessible and very pleasant.

Oregon Backroads Guide to the Pacific Crest Trail

The crystalline waters of the Wood River come bubbling from volcanic rocks and form this ice-cold pool.

The trail to the Wood River Springs is on the right as you enter the camp. Follow the short trail upstream and discover where the crystalline waters of the Wood River actually come bubbling forth. The multiple springs flow from the jumbled volcanic rocks, forming an ice-cold pool crossed by a wooden footbridge. The park is lightly used and a great place to camp just a few miles outside of Crater Lake National Park.

Highway 62 West from Fort Klamath Town: It's a short drive to the Park boundary from Fort Klamath.

Annie Creek Rest Area: Located just before the Park boundary and still in the Winema National Forest, this designated rest area and sno-park has an informal camp below the rest area. Follow the dirt road leading downhill from the parking area about a block to the camp on the banks of ice cold Annie Creek. There are no services here and no fees for camping. No restrooms at the camp, so just take the short walk back to the rest area to do any "resting."

Region 3 — Fort Klamath to Lemolo Lake

MAP R3.2: CRATER LAKE

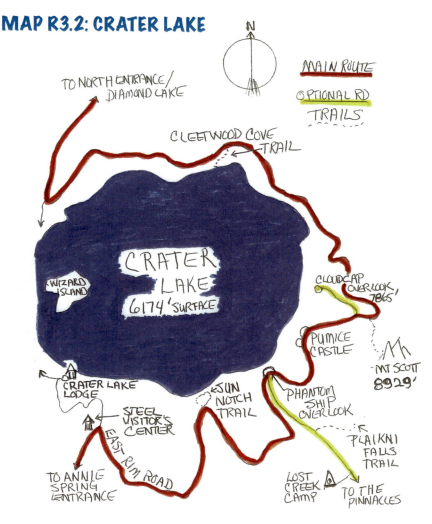

CRATER LAKE NATIONAL PARK

The Oregon Backroads Guide to the Pacific Crest Trail (and its humble author) would like to take this opportunity to apologize to those map readers who've noticed that the PCT traverses the west side of the park while the Guide suggests the east side of the park as the "Main Route" (marked in RED on the Guide Map).

While this may seem an egregious affront to the Guide's stated goal of providing a road trip version of the Pacific Crest Trail… May I point out that purists of the PCT have long bemoaned the fact that the official trail was routed well below the rim of the caldera with nary a glimpse of the lake. While travelers with stock must stay to the lower route, backpackers have the option of hiking up to the **Crater Lake Lodge** and staying on or near the west rim of the caldera as they make their way north to the junction of the two trails.

While it's certainly a plus for backpackers on the PCT to experience this visual treasure, the network of footpaths (and a stint on the pavement) goes through the most heavily traveled (and very beautiful nonetheless) part of the park with attendant crowds of people and cars as part of the scenery. If you have the time and the weather is nice, it's much better (me thinks) to take the Backroads, the way less traveled. It's probably genetic (I got it from my Dad), but I like the quieter side of Crater Lake National Park.

Views to the north of Crater Lake Lodge include Wizard Island.

Region 3 — Fort Klamath to Lemolo Lake

The East Rim Drive reaches its highest point at Cloudcap Overlook.

The **West Rim Road** is certainly worth driving and if time is short, it's the quickest way to the Park's North Junction Road and the exit via the North Entrance Station.

Annie Spring Entrance Station: From here it's 3.8 miles to the Steel Visitors Center and our turnoff to the East Rim Drive.

Pay the entrance fee ($10 as of 2014) and enter Oregon's only National Park. Long lines can form at the park entrance on summer days; it's best to get there extra early to avoid the crowds during the peak season. The **PCT** lies about a half-mile west of the entrance along Highway 62.

Dogs are mostly restricted from trails in the National Park. Pets are allowed within 50 feet of roads and other developed areas but are not allowed in the backcountry or other trails with the exception of the Old Grayback Road, connecting Vidae Falls and Lost Creek Campground.

Mazama Village Campground: The word village is perhaps an understatement… Operated by the park's concessionaire, Xanterra Parks and Resorts, this small town has

40 rooms in its motor lodge (called "The Cabins"), a grocery store, restaurant, gift shop, gas station, extensive campground with 212 sites, post office, ATM, laundry facilities, and showers. The **Annie Creek Restaurant** is open 7:00 a.m. until 9:00 p.m. during the summer.

Tent sites are $21 per night; RV sites with electrical hook-ups are $35. About three-fourths of the campsites can be reserved July through September. For further information and to make reservations, call 1-888-774-2728 or visit their website: craterlakelodges.com. Call the campground directly during the summer at 541-594-2255 ext. 3610.

CRATER LAKE N.P. HEADQUARTERS & VISITORS CENTER/EAST RIM DRIVE INTERSECTION: From here the Main Route turns right onto East Rim Drive; it's 2.9 miles to Vidae Falls.

Steel Visitors' Center: The visitors' center has the usual touristy stuff. There's a good selection of books and maps, hoodies, and coffee mugs.

Open year-round, the Steel Visitors' Center has the usual tourist items and educational displays, including a video worth watching.

Region 3 — Fort Klamath to Lemolo Lake

Vidae Falls is just 2.9 miles from the Steel Visitors' Center.

Take the time to watch the new (as of 2013) slickly produced 22-minute video. Shown every half-hour, it's about a variety of subjects including recent and ongoing research projects in the park. Along with amazing underwater scenes and cool 3-D effects, the video offers stunning scenic shots of the park. Narrated by Peter Coyote with a background of mesmerizing music, the video is entertaining and informative. The opening time-lapse scene of the night sky above the caldera rim is worth the price ($0) of admission.

To drive up to the caldera rim and Crater Lake Lodge from the visitor center, stay left at the intersection as the road heads north (uphill). The Main Route (marked in red on the Guide's Crater Lake Map) follows the East Rim Drive from Steel Visitors' Center. It's 2.9 miles to Vidae Falls.

HIGHLIGHTS OF THE EAST RIM DRIVE: Featuring some jaw dropping scenery, it's about 23 miles to North Junction from the Steel Visitors' Center. Add 12 miles if you choose to take the Pinnacles Road for a total of 35 miles. There are more than 20 pullouts along East Rim Drive. The road in places is a bit beat-up from the combination of weather and the annual pummeling of snowplows. Allow 2–3 hours to drive the Rim Drive and Pinnacles Road.

Vidae Falls: From here it's 1.3 miles to the Sun Notch parking area.

Falling over a series of rocky ledges this small but beautiful, spring-fed fall tumbles more than 100 feet to a lush flower-lined pool. Be careful not to trample the fragile plant growth if you choose to explore closer.

Sun Notch: From here its 3.9 miles to the **Phantom Ship Overlook** and **Pinnacles Road intersection**.

It's a short hike up to the notch and well worth the time. The trail is hard packed and achievable in a wheelchair with assistance. This is a great place to take first-time visitors for their initial glimpse of Crater Lake. This easy hike through several acres of wildflowers forms a loop back to the parking lot; allow 30–40 minutes.

The short hike up to Sun Notch is worthwhile for the close-up view of the Phantom Ship.

Region 3 — Fort Klamath to Lemolo Lake

View of Mt. Thielsen above the caldera rim.

When **Mt. Mazama** was whole, it stood thousands of feet higher than now. Before the eruptions that led up to the formation of the lake, glaciers flowing from ancient (12,000 ft. tall) Mt. Mazama carved a valley on this southern side between **Applegate Peak** and **Vidae Ridge** to the west and **Dutton Ridge** to our east.

After the summit collapsed (apparently in a matter of hours) about 7,700 years ago, this beheaded valley, itself choked with smoking debris, became a notch in the rim of the resulting **caldera** (Spanish for cauldron). Gaze at the scene across the lake and marvel at the other (less dramatic) glacial notches carved into ancient Mt. Mazama before the paroxysm.

Imagine how the post-eruption, rock-strewn, sheer-cliffed (3,000 ft. below our present viewpoint) volcanic cauldron below us would have looked before it cooled enough to fill with water. With steaming vents and rocks glowing red at night, it must have been an awesome sight indeed to anyone brave enough to sneak a peek. Nobody is sure exactly how long it was before the cauldron began to fill with water, but it was probably several centuries after the eruption before the lake appeared as it does today.

The views are stunning to the north where distant Mount Thielsen can be seen above the caldera rim. Various overlooks along the trail provide a good view of the Phantom Ship, anchored a thousand feet below us.

Back on the rim road we skirt south around Dutton Ridge and admire views far to the south of the Upper Klamath Basin, Pelican Butte, Mt. McLoughlin, and all the way to Mt. Shasta in California. Closer up (a few miles to the southwest) we'll see 7,709 ft. Union Peak, the central plug of an ancient Cascade volcano.

The forests to the east seem to blend into the horizon from this vantage point and 8,929-ft. Mt. Scott towers before us as the road bends northeast. The road turns north (with a good photo opportunity of Mt. Scott) and we soon arrive at the Phantom Ship/Pinnacles Road intersection.

PHANTOM SHIP/PINNACLES RD. INTERSECTION
Phantom Ship Overlook is located at this intersection.

Phantom Ship Overlook: This place above the rim is also known as **Kerr Notch**, the head of another decapitated glacial valley. Those of you that took the Sun Notch hike have already spied the Phantom Ship up close. This turnout has an interesting perspective across the lake of not only the Phantom Ship but also the western side of the caldera featuring Wizard Island and its 6,940-ft. cone, 8,151 ft. Hillman Peak to the left, and the tiny appearing lookout atop the 8,013 ft. Watchman on the rim to the right of the island.

From here it's 6 miles to the optional **Pinnacles Overlook trailhead**.

⇨ **Special Note:** *To skip the Pinnacles Road, see below at "Back on the Rim Road."*

The Pinnacles Road: Head 6 miles downhill (yeah, I know the sign says 7 miles) to the **Pinnacles Overlook** and trailhead. A parking area here has informational signs and vault toilets. A

Region 3 — Fort Klamath to Lemolo Lake

Hoodoo formations at the Pinnacles viewing area.

trail leaves the parking lot on the south side following the bluff for more views and in a short way to the park boundary.

The Pinnacles: Some of these striking stone formations stand 90 to 100 feet tall. They were formed into more erosion resistant rock than the ash and pumice surrounding them by the interaction of gases escaping from the hot materials buried here after the eruption of Mt. Mazama. Subsequently eroded away by wind and water in the ensuing thousands of years, the softer material has moved downhill leaving the striking **hoodoos** behind. Many of the spires have been found to be hollow like chimneys, apparently formed by the pressure of the escaping gases.

On the way to the Pinnacles we encounter **Plaikni Falls Trailhead** on our left.

Plaikni Falls: This easy, hard-packed trail is a pleasant 2.2-mile roundtrip walk through scattered forests of mountain hemlock and noble fir to an impressive spring-fed waterfall. It's a relatively new addition to the Park's hiking options, opening

Taking a break at Plaikni Falls.

in 2012. The first three-quarters of a mile or so is navigable in a wheelchair with assistance and features a view of the creek below the trail. The steeper ascent to the falls is probably not advisable for wheelchairs.

Originating at **Anderson Springs** at about 7,000 ft. elevation, Sand Creek takes a tumble over a glacier-carved ledge, creating a beautiful spray garden of wildflowers in the summer. **Plaikni** is a native word interpreted as "from the high mountains." Continuing downhill on the Pinnacles Road, we come to Lost Creek Campground on our right.

Lost Creek Campground: Located on the flats separating spring-fed Lost Creek and impressively eroded Sand Creek on the other side of the road, the campground is operated by the National Forest Service and has 16 sites catering to tent campers only. This is the only car camp in the park boundaries.

Although not what you'd call scenic, it's near enough to several hiking trails, including the old gravel Grayback Road, which is closed to motorized travel and the only substantial area in the

Region 3 — Fort Klamath to Lemolo Lake

Pumice Castle guards the flanks of Crater Lake.

park open to pets. With water and flush toilets it's only $10 a night. Each site has a fire ring, picnic table, and steel bear locker.

It's first come, first served with no reservations taken, so get here early (and bring plenty of DEET in the early season) if you expect to find an open site.

BACK ON THE RIM ROAD: After leaving the Pinnacles Road intersection and heading east on the Rim Road, it's two miles to the first in a series of four overlooks at Castle Rock and Pumice Castle.

Pumice Castle: Stop at the **Pumice Castle Overlook** and gaze at the orange-colored pumice rock that has eroded into shapes resembling a turreted medieval castle carved into the caldera wall. From here it's about 1.5 miles to the turnoff to **Cloudcap Overlook** and the **Mt. Scott trailhead**.

Cloudcap Overlook: It's about a mile up to the overlook from the Rim Road. At 7,865 ft. elevation this is the highest road-accessible point in the park and purportedly the highest paved road in Oregon. The scene from here is of course stunning on a clear day. The layered structure of old Mt. Mazama is very evident and the views of the surrounding country go on for a hundred miles or more. Soak up the views across the lake, then take a look up the hill behind the parking area at the gnarled **whitebark pines** that cling to survival in this harsh and windy environment.

Mount Scott Trailhead: Gaining 1,250 feet in elevation in 2.5 miles, the 5 miles roundtrip trail to the lookout is mostly a gradual ascent with the exception of a series of switchbacks as it works its way up to the summit ridge. The trail is listed as strenuous largely because of the elevation; the trailhead is above 7,500 feet! Allow about 3 hours for the hike.

Typical snow years find the trail open in mid-July. Take plenty of water and your camera. The views of the lake from the top are best under morning light. Because of this volcano's position on the east side of the park, the amazing views up and down the Cascade Range and the endless valleys and forests to the east, combine for breathtaking scenery.

The gnarled whitebark pines provide shelter from the wind and shade from the sun at this picnic area with a view.

Region 3 — Fort Klamath to Lemolo Lake

Visible from the East Rim Drive, Mt. Scott is a volcanic satellite cone that pre-dates Mt. Mazama's eruption.

Mt. Scott, elevation 8,929 ft., is the highest point in the park and the largest of the several surviving satellite cones pre-dating the eruption of Mt. Mazama. These parasitic cones may have contributed to the engulfment of Mt. Mazama by tapping into the magma chamber beneath the mountain, helping to evacuate the molten rock before the summit's collapse.

Mt. Scott's western side was heavily eroded by glaciers leaving no trace of a summit cone. Ice flowing down from ancient Mt. Mazama met the obstacle of Mt. Scott and gouged deeply into its northwestern slope. It's clear that this happened previous to the destruction of Mt. Mazama's summit so Mt. Scott was apparently fully formed previous to the creation of the caldera and is now probably extinct.

Back on the Rim Road heading north, we find the **Whitebark Pine Picnic Area**, a pleasant circle of beautifully wind sculpted whitebarks with picnic tables and great views of Mt. Scott. From here it's about 2.5 miles to the **Lake in Legend Overlook**.

Oregon Backroads Guide to the Pacific Crest Trail

Look closely; the two tiny white dots on the lake are excursion boats, carrying 37 passengers each, that depart from Cleetwood Cove.

The Lake in Legend Overlook: The informational boards at this overlook illustrate the **Native American** legends surrounding the caldera's creation. Passed on through the generations of people who no doubt witnessed the eruption, many American Native people still live in the area. The National Park allows native groups to use the park for educational and ceremonial purposes today.

From the overlook it's 4.0 miles to the **Cleetwood Cove Trailhead**.

Cleetwood Cove Trailhead: Only 1.1 miles to the lake? That sounds easy enough, right?…Before you decide to hike the trail though, spend a few minutes at the trailhead to look at the pain etched in (even young) people's faces as they climb the last few yards back to the road. If you decide to hike the trail, bring water and wear good shoes.

The parking lot fills up fast on summer weekends; get there early to buy your ticket for the boat tour. Each of the motor launches holds 37 passengers and tickets are best purchased in advance to guarantee seats. Call 1-888-774-2728 to reserve tickets.

Region 3 — Fort Klamath to Lemolo Lake

If a tour doesn't sell out, tickets can be purchased at the Cleetwood Cove ticket booth for tours leaving in 45 minutes (or up to 2 hrs. 45 min. before departure) to allow time to walk the trail down to the boat landing. Swimming and fishing are allowed at **Cleetwood Cove** and **Wizard Island**.

To spend time at Wizard Island and hike to the island's cinder cone summit, make arrangements when booking your reservation. Take plenty of water and food, bring sun protection like sunscreen and a hat, wear sturdy boots, and bring a warm, rain-resistant jacket.

North Junction: From here it's about 9 miles north to Highway 138 and our turnoff to Diamond Lake. This is the junction of the East Rim Drive and the West Rim Drive; turn south and arrive at the Crater Lake Lodge in 6 miles.

Pumice Desert: This stark landscape also provides a dramatic view of another of the several parasitic volcanoes related to the Mt. Mazama complex. The aptly (if unimaginatively) named Red Cone is relatively young and may have been active within the last few thousand years.

The pumice desert supports hardy, drought-resistant plant life.

The so-called Pumice Desert is slowly being colonized by high mountain plants and animals. Although covered by several feet of snow in the winter, the porous nature of the pumice creates "desert like" conditions after the snow melts and the rain stops. What appears as barren ground from a distance on closer examination reveals a few ground-hugging and drought-tolerant plants making a living here.

North Entrance Station: The North Entrance is closed no later than November 1st and is the principal way into the park for snowmobiles during the winter and early spring months. Contact **Diamond Lake Resort** (see below) for more information on booking snowmobile tours.

HIGHWAY 138 TO HIGHWAY 230 INTERSECTION:

After passing the North Entrance station, we'll turn left and head west on Highway 138. Heading downhill on Highway 138 we spy **Mt. Bailey** looming up from the west before getting a peek at Diamond Lake. After traveling about three miles, we come to the major intersection with Highway 230 and the sign pointing south towards Medford. Turn left at this intersection and head south towards Medford. Please read the Special Note! below.

Hwy 230 South Intersection:

- ⇨ **Special Note!** *This is the way south to Medford.* **We're on this road for about a city block** *before turning right (west) on the* **Diamond Lake Recreation Road***.*
- ⇨ **Special, Special Note!!** *Just another city block south on Highway 230 takes you to the* **Mt. Thielsen Viewpoint***. Don't miss it!*

Region 3 — Fort Klamath to Lemolo Lake

MAP R3.3: DIAMOND LAKE AREA

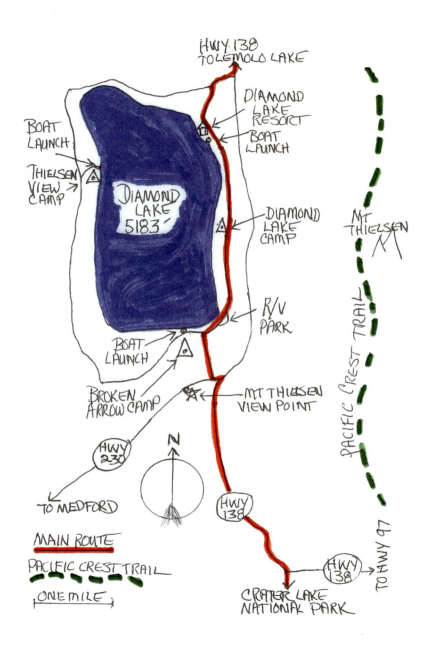

Diamond Lake is a great place for boating and fishing.

DIAMOND LAKE AREA

After turning off from Highway 230 we quickly arrive at an intersection where we'll keep to the right (north).

The lake covers over 2,800 acres and is about 50 feet at its deepest point. The paved **Dellenback Bike Trail** loops Diamond Lake and spans about 11 miles of mostly level pavement for bikers and hikers too; just follow the bicycle icons through the campgrounds.

In the summer, stop at the **South Shore Pizza Parlor** along the way for food and perhaps a beer. With a great selection of microbrews, they also have a growler station, (a growler is a refillable glass container for to-go beer) and that's right…pizza!

Diamond Lake itself is largely the product of Mt. Mazama and its subsequent eruption over 7,700 years ago. Pre-eruption, 12,000-foot Mt. Mazama had extensive glaciers, and one of these northward moving mountains of ice scooped out the valley between 9,182-foot **Mt. Thielsen** to the east and the younger volcano, 8,363-foot **Mt. Bailey** to the west.

Region 3 — Fort Klamath to Lemolo Lake

When Mt. Mazama erupted, it partially filled this valley with volcanic debris and formed a dike of pyroclastic material blocking the outlet of the drainage. Water quickly filled the resulting depression, and a shallow lake was formed. Finding an eventual outlet along the rocky ledge at today's Lake Creek, Diamond Lake, "the Gem of the Cascades," came into being.

Fishing can be good and trout in the five- to ten-pound range are boated here annually. This natural lake and healthy food chain produces clouds of insects and aquatic critters that grow trout big and fat.

Take warning of the clouds of insects (skeeters) that can be present here just after ice off in the late spring and early summer. These persistent devils want to include your blood in the food chain. Hardy early season fishers and campers bring warm clothes and lots of DEET... August and September are the best times to camp here.

MOUNT BAILEY: Elevation 8,364 ft.

Mount Bailey stands guard over the western side of Diamond Lake. Revered by the Native Americans who lived in the area,

Mt. Bailey and its reflection in Diamond Lake.

its name in the native tongue translates to "Medicine Mountain." Legend tells us that chiefs and medicine men held ritual feasts atop the volcano.

The trail to the summit is about 5 miles long and gains 3,000 feet; there's no water along the way. Starting out in the trees, the trail reaches the tree-line after about 4 miles. The last bit to the summit is steep and rocky. Look for the crater perched on the summit ridge. During the winter the volcano is a favorite among sno-cat skiers.

MOUNT THIELSEN: Elevation 9,182 ft.

This heavily eroded volcano stands astride the Cascade Crest. Easily seen from almost anywhere along the Crater Lake Rim Road, Mt. Thielsen arises from a broad plain to an almost sheer point east of Diamond Lake. The **Pacific Crest Trail** traverses the western slopes of this mountain.

With a striking obelisk marking the hardened plug of the ancient volcano (which originally stood more than 10,000 ft. tall) it's easy to see why this probably extinct mountain is called

Mt. Thielsen stands astride the Cascade Crest and is known as the "Lightning Rod of the Cascades."

Region 3 — Fort Klamath to Lemolo Lake

The marina at Diamond Lake Resort.

the **"Lightning Rod of the Cascades."** Attracting innumerable lightning bolts over the millennia, repeated strikes on the summit have formed an odd substance called **fulgarite**. Derived from the Latin word *"fulmen"* meaning thunderbolts or lightning, fulgarite forms a glassy surface on the summit rocks by fusing crystalline materials existing in volcanic rocks.

Fulgarites can also be found in the cracks and crevices of the summit rocks. There's a 5-mile trail heading up the west side to the summit; an airy scramble with some alarming exposure gets you to the top. Watch out for fulmen…

Diamond Lake Resort (open 365 days a year) has facilities for weddings, conventions, and all sorts of other events.

Diamond Lake Resort:
541-793-3383 • diamond lake.net

They have a well stocked grocery store, post office, gas station, boat rentals, and a full service marina. With a capacity of over 300 guests, this is the mother of all southern Oregon mountain lake resorts. The resort rents cabins and motel rooms and has an extensive RV park (541-793-3318 or diamondlakervpark.com). It also has three restaurants, including the **South Shore Pizza Parlor**, the more upscale **Mt. Bailey Sports Grill and Lounge**, and the **Diamond Lake Café**. A full service cocktail lounge called the Diamond Room is upstairs.

The resort sponsors an annual fishing derby held in late June that attracts trout fisherman from near and far. On other summer weekends, the resort holds conventions for everyone from (I'm not making this up) square dancers to radiologists.

During the winter the resort hosts sled dog races and cross-country ski races. This is also prime country for snowshoeing and snowmobiling with over 300 miles of groomed trails with races and poker runs for both. The lake is entirely on **Umpqua National Forest** land so it's open to shore angling everywhere. Please use courtesy and common sense when accessing the lake shore.

Diamond Lake is open year-round for fishing with ice fishing in the winter. Check your local regulations.

The nearby **Diamond Lake Corrals** offers daily, guided trail rides ranging from one hour to all day and has corrals for rent with nearby camping for those bringing their own horses. Contact Diamond Lake Corrals at 541-793-3337 or 541-297-6095 or on the web at diamondlakecorrals.com.

For Forest Service campground information in the Diamond Lake area, call 541-793-3310 or 541-498-2531.

Diamond Lake Campground: This humongous campground has 239 fee sites laid out in linear fashion stretching almost two miles along the eastern shore of Diamond Lake. The various designated loops in the road layout use up a good portion of the alphabet starting with the letter "A" and ending with the letter "M." More then half of the campsites can be reserved by calling 1-877-444-6777 or on the web at recreation.gov. All other sites are first come, first served.

Region 3 — Fort Klamath to Lemolo Lake

The campground has two boat ramps and a fish cleaning station. There are showers, flush toilets, and RV dump station. It's $16 to camp inland; lakefront sites with views of Mt. Bailey and afternoon sun are $6 extra.

Broken Arrow Campground: Only half the size of Diamond Lake Campground, Broken Arrow has a measly 117 fee sites located inland from the south shore of the lake; it's $15 for family sites. It's about a half-mile to the **South Shore Day-Use Area** and **boat launch**.

Each campsite has tables and fire rings and some can accommodate trailers to 35 ft. There are flush toilets and showers accessible to wheelchairs. Most sites are first come, first served with reservations available for some group sites through recreation.gov

Thielsen View Campground: They don't call it Thielsen View for nothing you know…With 60 fee sites, water, boat ramp, vault toilets, and killer views of Mt. Thielsen, this heavily used, improved campground located on the northwest shore of the lake has nice waterfront exposure among the trees. It's $15 to camp here.

Thielsen View Campground is located across the lake from the resort along the #4795 Road. Heading north along this road, we come to the junction of the Resort Road and the **Diamond Lake Gas Station**. This is the best place to gas up if you're following the Guide through Region Four. The station is about two city blocks above Diamond Lake Resort and a city block downhill from Highway 138 and our turnoff northbound to Lemolo Lake intersection.

Oregon Backroads Guide to the Pacific Crest Trail

MAP R3.4: LEMOLO LAKE AREA

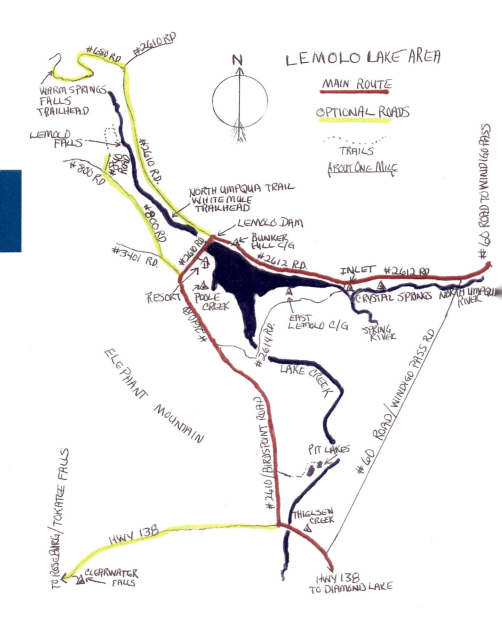

Region 3 — Fort Klamath to Lemolo Lake

NORTH ON HWY. 138 TO LEMOLO LAKE: Leaving the Diamond Lake area, we head north on Highway 138.

Thielsen Creek Forest Camp: Located alongside Highway 138 between Diamond Lake and the Lemolo Lake turnoff, Thielsen Creek Camp has been recently improved with vault toilets and fire rings. This rustic camp is just that, a few sites situated in the trees with little else; very suitable for deer camp in the fall or a spur of the moment overnight tent camp. No trailers. No fees as of 2013.

Lemolo Lake Intersection: Here we turn north on Road #2610 (The Birds Point Road) towards Lemolo Lake Resort to follow the Main Route.

To skip the **Optional Falls Tour**, go to the **"Pit Lakes Trail"** description below.

OPTIONAL FALLS TOUR: If we continue west on Highway 138 towards Roseburg, there are four beautiful waterfalls within 14 miles of this intersection. Although not on the official Main Route, I highly recommend taking the falls tour. Each of the four falls near Highway 138 described below has its own distinct personality. From the Lemolo Lake Intersection allow about 2 hours to explore and enjoy the four falls.

Two other nearby falls (Lemolo Falls and Warm Spring Creek Falls) northwest of Lemolo Lake **are described in Region Four** of this book.

Clearwater Falls: The first falls we encounter as we drive west on Highway 138 is on the Clearwater River. As the name implies, the waters of this river are exceedingly clear. Just a mile or so above the falls, the river emanates from pure springs flowing from a jumble of lava. The viewing area for the falls is a very short walk and wheelchair accessible. Adjacent to the parking area is a pleasant picnic area and informational signs.

Whitehorse Falls: Also on the Clearwater River, this pleasant fall is a very short walk from the parking area and has access to the pools below. The Whitehorse Campground (5 sites) is nearby.

Oregon Backroads Guide to the Pacific Crest Trail

Whitehorse Falls is a short walk from the parking area.

Watson Falls: From the parking area, it's about 0.3 miles to the falls viewing area. The trail is rather strenuous and immediately heads uphill following Watson Creek through lush glades and past sparkling pools. Typical of the western High Cascades, this area gets about 80 inches of precipitation annually. Look for wildflowers of all descriptions among the massive trees and moss-covered rocks below the spray pool. The falls push over a sheer columnar basalt cliff and descend 293 feet, making it the tallest waterfall in southwestern Oregon. Heading down from the viewing area, there's an alternate trail that follows the other side of the creek, making a short loop back to the parking area.

Informational signs in the parking area show some beautiful photos of the falls taken during winter along with general information about the local geology.

Tokatee Falls: The trail to the falls overlook is about 0.3 miles from the parking lot. As we pull into the parking area it's hard to ignore the huge wooden pipeline (called a

Region 3 — Fort Klamath to Lemolo Lake

Spray from 293-foot Watson Falls supports a lush forest along the trail.

"penstock") adjacent to the pavement. Made of redwood and banded together with metal staves, the penstock channels water under gravity pressure (squirting out in places) downhill from here to power turbines creating electricity. It's all part of Pacific Corps hydroelectric project on the North Umpqua, an extensive operation with eight dams and multiple generating stations.

The trail follows the **North Umpqua River** downstream (west) and after negotiating hundreds of steps (both uphill and downhill) you'll arrive at a wooden platform overlooking the falls. The platform is perched on a steep slope and wraps around a huge tree, giving it the feel of being high up in a tree house with an exquisite view. Soak up the awesome scene of the North Umpqua River as it falls over a series of basalt ledges before launching into space 80 feet above the splash pool.

Pit Lakes Trail: We get back on the Main Route and continue from the Lemolo Lake Intersection above.

Region 3 — Fort Klamath to Lemolo Lake

As we head north towards Lemolo Lake on the #2610 Road, a little less than a mile from the Highway 138 intersection, we'll see a dirt road to our right (east) marked with a hikers trail sign. Follow this road about a block and a half to the gated trailhead entrance. It's a short hike on the old road to the first of two lakes formed by past gravel mining operations here. Not much to look at, the first surprisingly deep lake holds some nice rainbow trout, up to about 15 inches. A quarter-mile past this is the second "pit" lake. Look for **osprey** nesting here in the surrounding trees.

Back on the main road, it's two miles north to the intersection of the #2610 and #2614 Roads.

#2614 Road Intersection: From here we continue north on the #2610/Birds Point Road towards Lemolo Lake Resort and the end of Region Three.

The road to our right (east) is the East Lemolo Lake Road and goes to East Lemolo Lake Campground, Inlet Campground, Crystal Springs, the road to Lake Timpanogas, and the Windigo Pass Road, all described in Region Four. Staying on the #2610 Road, it's about a mile to Poole Creek Campground.

Poole Creek Campground: With 59 fee sites, Poole Creek campground is located on the southwest shore of Lemolo Lake. This improved campground is much quieter then anything you'll find on more popular Diamond Lake. With water, vault toilets, garbage and recycling service, a boat ramp, and a beautiful day-use area, it can be downright peaceful here (and relatively bug free) in late August and early September. Heading north on the #2610 Road as we leave Poole Creek Campground, we quickly encounter an intersection to our left (west). This is the #3401 Road and leads to the trailhead (on the #840 Rd.) to beautiful **Lemolo Falls**, described in Region Four.

Staying north on Road #2610, we soon arrive at the turnoff to Lemolo Lake Resort and the end of Region Three.

⇐   *The dramatic scene of Tokatee Falls plummeting 80 feet to the river below.*

Oregon Backroads Guide to the Pacific Crest Trail

An osprey fishing at Poole Creek Campground swimming area, Lemolo Lake.

END OF REGION THREE

In Region Three we started out on the headwaters of the Klamath River in Eastern Oregon, traveled through Oregon's only National Park and past beautiful Diamond Lake. The end of Region Three finds us in western Oregon and near the headwaters of the mighty Umpqua River, near Lemolo Lake.

Looking ahead to Region Four, we'll explore the Lemolo Lake area, cross the **Calapooya Divide** to the headwaters of the storied Willamette River and then on to eastern Oregon and the top of the **Deschutes River** drainage. After passing by three large natural lakes, Region Four ends at **Willamette Pass**. We'll have lots of opportunity for boating, fishing, hiking, and camping along the way, of course. Have fun!

There are **no services between Lemolo Lake and Crescent Lake Junction** so go prepared.

REGION FOUR
Lemolo Lake to Odell Lake

Region Four offers many opportunities for boating and fishing.

"I'm walking down the Backroads of my mind, strolling through the Kaleidoscope of inner space and time."
— Electric Apricot/Les Claypool

The single campsite at serene Linda Lake marks the trailhead to more lakes. ⇨

Region 4 — Lemolo Lake to Odell Lake

ROUTE DESCRIPTION

This part of our journey begins at Lemolo Lake, heads north over the Calapooya Mountains, skirts Crescent and Odell Lakes and ends at Willamette Pass. The Main Route travels past four additional lakes and through some of the least traveled areas of the central Cascades. The optional roads lead to two waterfalls near Lemolo Lake (with short hikes), and for low-clearance vehicles, across Windigo Pass to Crescent Lake. Total distance is 50 to 65 miles.

⇨ **Lemolo Lake Resort is the last place to gas up before Crescent Lake Junction.**

⇨ **Allow 6 to 8 hours with several stops.**

ROAD CONDITIONS

Most of the Region Four route is paved with about 20 miles of dirt road **(not plowed in the winter)** regardless of the route chosen. The **optional dirt road across Windigo Pass** is suitable for any vehicle with reasonable clearance.

Of the 20 miles of dirt road in the Main Route, all of it is improved and suitable for any vehicle **with the exception of the #6010 Road around Summit Lake.** The #6010 Road connecting Summit Lake with Crescent Lake **should only be attempted by high-clearance vehicles.**

Contact the Crescent Ranger Station at 503-433-2234 for roads in the Deschutes National Forest. Call the Diamond Lake Ranger Station at 541-498-2531 for road information in the Umpqua National Forest.

MAPS FOR REGION FOUR

The Umpqua National Forest, Diamond Lake Ranger District, and Deschutes National Forest maps are available on-line at fs.usda.gov. Look for Benchmark maps at your local outdoor retailer or order on-line at benchmarkmaps.com.

Oregon Backroads Guide to the Pacific Crest Trail

Maps recommended for Region Four are listed below
- Umpqua National Forest Map
- Diamond Lake Ranger District Map
- Deschutes National Forest Map
- Benchmark Maps – *Oregon Road and Recreation Atlas* – page 73

MAIN ROADS IN ORDER OF TRAVEL
All Regional Routes are listed South to North.

#2610/Birds Point Rd.	The paved connection from Hwy. 138 to Lemolo Resort.
#60/Windigo Pass	We're on the #60 Rd. for 2.3 miles before turning on the #700 Rd.
#700 Rd.	The gravel road past Linda Lake.
#770 Rd.	This gravel road takes us over Calapooya Gap, becomes the #2154 Rd.
#2154 Rd.	Gravel road takes us past Timpanogas and Opal Lakes.
#6010 Rd.	The rough road connection between Summit Lake and Crescent Lake.
#60 Rd.	The paved road around Crescent Lake.
Hwy. 58	The State Highway takes us to Willamette Pass from Crescent Lake Junction.

OPTIONAL ROADS
Roads are also described in the Road Notes.

#3401 Rd.	The improved gravel road connects with the #800 Rd.
#800 Rd.	The gravel road connects with the #840 Rd.
#840 Rd.	The short road to Lemolo Falls trailhead.
Windigo Pass Rd.	This is the #60 Rd. and is for low-clearance vehicles

Region 4 — Lemolo Lake to Odell Lake

MAP R4.1: MAIN ROUTE

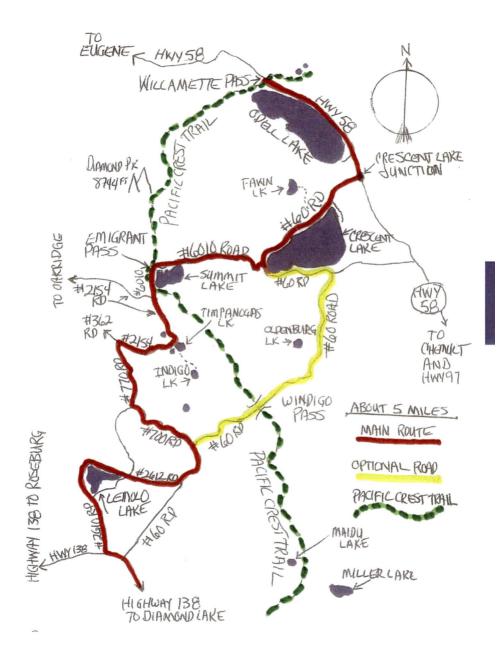

ROAD NOTES REGION FOUR

Starting at Lemolo Lake, the Region Four Route stays in the High Cascades, ending at Willamette Pass. The following notes describe the sights and attractions along the way.

Lemolo Lake Area: It's a pretty little (out of the way) spot among the pines with Mt. Thielsen framing the eastern skyline. Who could ask for more?

Lemolo Lake is part of Pacific Corp's hydro-electric project on the North Umpqua Basin. Formed by a dam on the upper river, the 415-acre lake provides fishing and recreation opportunities.

Served by four National Forest Campgrounds and a resort, the lake is a more sedate alternative to Diamond Lake in the summer. Boat ramps are located at the resort, East Lemolo Lake Campground, and Poole Creek Campground. A few informal camps along the northern shore of the lake offer camping right on the lake, and a couple of boat-in sites are available elsewhere on the lake.

*Stonecrop (*Sedum divergens*) is a rock-loving plant that stores water in its leaves. Found near Lemolo Lake.*

Region 4 — Lemolo Lake to Odell Lake

MAP R4.2: LEMOLO LAKE AREA

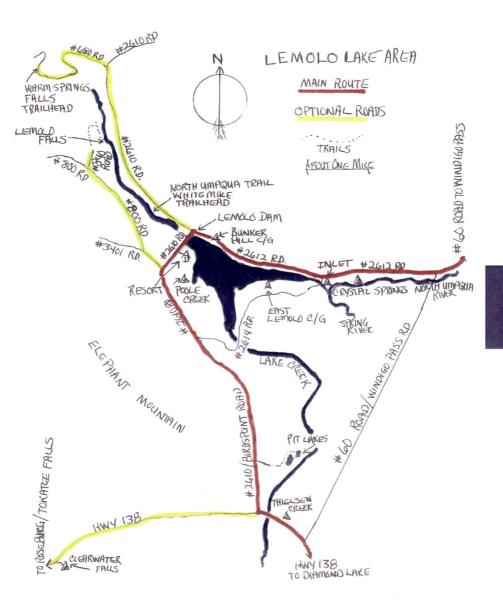

It's good, clean fun at Lemolo Lake Resort.

Make sure you bring your sense of humor when checking in at the **Lemolo Lake Resort**, the cafe offers a Sunday morning brunch with a sign advising "all you can stand" for $9. The coffee is good and strong, guaranteed to snap your eyes open so hard it'll leave a dent on your forehead, or your money back.

Lemolo Lake Resort:

2610 Birds Point Road • 541-643-0750 • lemololakeresort.com

Located near the dam on the northeast side of the lake, "Good Clean Fun" is the motto at Lemolo Lake Resort. With a cafe and store, boat rentals, marina, cabins, and an RV park the resort caters to fishermen in search of the big brown trout (30 inches plus) that inhabit these sparkling waters. Grab your fly rod and fish from a float tube in the inlets early in the morning for a chance at the big browns. Fishing for rainbow and kokanee and boating of all sorts, including pontoon boats, canoeing and kayaking fill in the summer season.

Like Lemolo Lake itself, the resort is laid back and quiet, especially during the late part of the season. The resort and the surrounding National Forest campgrounds can get busy in August

Region 4 — Lemolo Lake to Odell Lake

(before school but after mosquitoes). After Labor Day, the rhythm slows and September usually brings sunny and warm weather.

The store has an impressive selection of books and maps of the region along with camper's supplies and fishing gear. The owners and staff are happy to offer advice and show you the various set-ups commonly used to fish the lake.

The resort has been active in creating a trophy brown trout fishery at Lemolo and recommends releasing the larger browns. There's a big wooden table adjacent to the fireplace in the common area of the lodge where tall tales (and fishing stories) are told regularly…

The RV park has 20 sites, all with full hook-ups for $30 per night. The cabins rent from $150 per night. There are also 4 motel rooms from $89 per night.

TRAILS IN THE LEMOLO AREA

If you make your base at Lemolo Lake, you'll find plenty of trails to hike, including the Lemolo Falls Trail, the North Umpqua Trail complex, and the Warm Spring Creek Fall Trail.

Look for trilliums on the Lemolo Falls Trail.

Oregon Backroads Guide to the Pacific Crest Trail

A luscious splash pool at the bottom of Lemolo Falls rewards hikers who opt to take the mile-long trail.

Lemolo Falls Trail: So what's your idea of the perfect waterfall? Perhaps it's the tropical version with beautiful wildflowers, ferns, and towering rocky cliffs?

Well strap on your daypack and check these falls out on a midsummer morning. Sure the temp might be in the 50s but the ferns, beautiful wildflowers, and rocky cliffs are there... The North Umpqua trail follows the north side of the river and provides views down into the canyon near the falls, but there's no trail down to the falls from that side.

Instead, take the #3401 Road (marked in yellow on the Guide map) to the #800 Road; turn right (north) on the #840 Road to the trailhead parking lot. It's about a mile from the parking lot to the end of the trail. The trail descends along an old roadbed to an ancient car camp, complete with ancient picnic table.

From there the trail descends the river's canyon in one long switchback, arriving at a good view as the full force of the North Umpqua River plummets more than 100 feet before rejoining the river below. The formal trail ends here but those

Region 4 — Lemolo Lake to Odell Lake

more adventurous (or foolish) can scramble over the slippery moss covered rocks to the foot of the falls.

North Umpqua Trail: Beginning in the early 1970s, trails advocates promoted the construction of a trail that would connect the Lower North Umpqua with its ultimate source at Maidu Lake, high in the Cascades. Completed in 1997, the 79-mile trail takes hikers, fishers, cyclists, and horsemen through several stands of old growth trees, a hot spring, and past waterfalls galore.

Twelve main trailheads provide access to trail segments varying in length from 3.5 miles to over 15 miles. The Swiftwater Trailhead on the lower river stands at just over 800 feet in elevation. As the path heads east, it steadily gains elevation, topping out at 6,000 feet near Maidu Lake.

The **White Mule Trailhead** near Lemolo Lake is at 3,920 feet. Head west along the "Dread and Terror" segment to Umpqua Hot Springs and you'll travel about 13 miles while losing 1,200 feet in elevation. Travel east 6.3 miles from White Mule and you'll gain 360 feet in elevation to the next trailhead at Kelsay Horse Camp. From the horse camp the path crosses into the Mt. Thielsen Wilderness and ends near the Cascade Crest at **Maidu Lake**, about 9 miles from Kelsay Horse Camp.

Warm Spring Creek Fall Trail: Hike this short, wheelchair friendly trail and find a beautiful waterfall cascading over a row of basalt columns. Warm Spring Creek flows well, even in the heat of summer. The creek has carved a niche through the solid basalt and presents a striking scene among the massive trees and mossy rocks. The viewing area is above the steep-sided creek bed with no practical way down to the base of the falls, so enjoy your picnic there.

To drive to the trailhead from Lemolo Lake Resort, head north on the #2610 Road across the dam. Past the dam the road splits with the #2610 Road turning left (heading west — marked in yellow on the Guide map) and the Main Route (marked in red on the Guide map) #2612 Road turning right (heading east) towards Windigo Pass.

Region 4 — Lemolo Lake to Odell Lake

Stay left on the paved #2610 Road for about 3 miles to the first major intersection on the left. Here we'll turn left (west) on the gravel #680 Road. The road switchbacks as it heads downhill and in about 2 miles, we come to the small parking area and marked trailhead on our left.

CAMPGROUNDS IN THE LEMOLO LAKE AREA

Several campgrounds are available in the Lemolo Lake region, including Poole Creek, East Lemolo Campground, Inlet Campground, and Crystal Spring Campground.

Poole Creek Campground: This campground is described in Region Three, and has the capacity to launch larger boats.

Bunker Hill Campground: Located above the north shore of Lemolo Lake, this small campground has 6 fee sites and is best suited to tent campers and those with small RVs. Turn-around space is limited so this camp will not accommodate big trailers. The campground has vault toilets and water. There's no road connection to the lake here but a short hike leads down to water's edge and a pleasant beach when the lake's full.

East Lemolo Campground: While there's an official boat launch here, it's best suited to smaller boats. The boat launch is more useful when the lake is full. A few of the campsites have waterfront where a boat can be brought to shore. Some folks with bigger boats launch at Poole Creek or the resort and tie-up here. East Lemolo has 15 fee sites, vault toilets, and water. It's $10 to camp here.

Inlet Campground: Above this campground several springs contribute their waters to the North Umpqua as it flows into Lemolo Lake. The Spring River and Crystal Springs provide ice-cold waters to the reservoir regardless of the season. The kokanee (land-locked salmon) follow their primal urges and flash spawning colors during their September and October foray into Spring River.

⇐ *Warm Springs Creek Falls near Lemolo Lake.*

Waiting below at the confluence, the big browns gulp up any love drunk kokanee that dance their way. This is also the time fishermen target the trout where the North Umpqua merges into the lake. Inlet has 14 fee sites, and vault toilets, but no boat launch. It's $10 to camp here.

In June and July, the riparian area along the North Umpqua is a great place to look for **common paintbrush** (*Castilleja miniata*). With around 200 species of castilleja occurring worldwide, almost 40 varieties live in the northwestern United States and Canada. Called the common paintbrush and coincidentally the most common paintbrush at mid-elevation areas of the Oregon Cascades, these sturdy water lovers can grow to 3 feet tall. The **Indian paintbrush** (*Castilleja hispida*) can be more often found at higher elevations. This version of paintbrush is brilliantly red and tends to be more low-growing.

Crystal Spring: Located east of Inlet Campground and just below the #2612 Road, a single informal campsite adjacent to the springs allows access. The multiple, ice-cold springs

An informal campground on the North Umpqua River.

Region 4 — Lemolo Lake to Odell Lake

This example of common paintbrush was found at East Lemolo Campground.

flow from the hillside and are major contributors to the North Umpqua. To the southeast, the much bigger spring forming the headwaters of the Spring River comes bubbling forth from the rocks and joins the North Umpqua River nearby.

#2612 ROAD & #60 ROAD INTERSECTION:

⇨ **Special Note!** *The* Main Route *heads north on the #60 Road for only 2.3 miles before turning west on the #700 Road* (consult the Guide map). *Look for the turnoff to the #700 Road to your left. The #700 Road may not be signed but it's a wide, gravel road heading uphill across the road from a large informational sign. The sign at the turn-off says Windigo Pass is 5 miles north. The road across* **Windigo Pass is the optional road***, best for low-clearance vehicles.*

For those following the Main Route*, continue below at, "Heading Northwest on the #700 Road."*

★ 155 ★

Oregon Backroads Guide to the Pacific Crest Trail

MAP R4.3: HEADING NORTH FROM LEMOLO LAKE

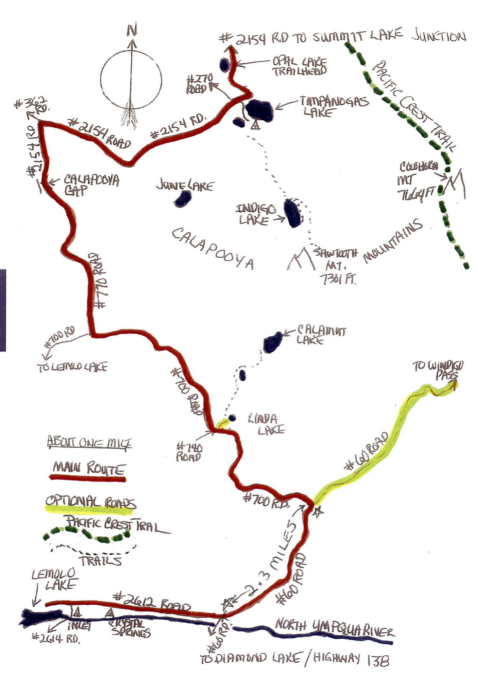

Region 4 — Lemolo Lake to Odell Lake

OPTIONAL #60 ROAD ACROSS WINDIGO PASS:

⇨ **Note! Windigo Pass Road crests the Cascades at over 5,800 feet and is not plowed in the winter. The pass is typically closed by snow (at least to wheeled vehicles) from November through late spring or early summer.**

From the intersection of the #2612 Road and the Windigo Pass Road, it's a total of 16 miles to the stop sign near Crescent Lake. If you choose to take this optional road, you will stay on the #60 Road to its intersection with Highway 58 at Crescent Lake Junction.

It's probably safe to say that of all the improved road passes in the Cascades, Windigo Pass is the second least traveled (after Griffin Pass described in Region Two of this guide). Like Griffin Pass, the Windigo Road #60 essentially goes north-south but divides Western Oregon from Eastern Oregon. From the south near Lemolo Lake the #60 Road heads north and takes travelers from the Umpqua drainage into the Deschutes River drainage near Crescent Lake.

The Windigo Pass Route rejoins the Main Route near Spring Campground on Crescent Lake. That's Diamond Peak in the background.

Oregon Backroads Guide to the Pacific Crest Trail

MAP R4.4: OPTIONAL WINDIGO PASS ROUTE

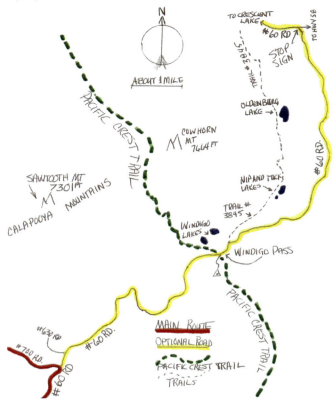

The road is washboarded and heads steadily uphill as we leave the North Umpqua and travel northeast on the #60 Road, attaining the summit in about 7.5 miles.

At the Windigo Pass Summit, elevation 5,824 feet, we intersect the **Pacific Crest Trail.** From the summit, the #501 Road heads south (uphill). Soon it comes to an unmarked campground. With fire rings and a couple of picnic tables, this spot is used by PCT hikers, horse campers, and car campers alike.

As we head downhill on the #60 Road, it becomes narrower and mildly rutted but any car will do; a half-mile below the pass we come to another trailhead on our left. This is the **#3845 Trail** (Oldenburg Lake trail), used by PCT hikers as an alternate to the main route mostly because the main route is waterless for many miles north.

Region 4 — Lemolo Lake to Odell Lake

After leaving the trailhead, the road widens and becomes less steep as it makes its way north to the stop sign, 8.6 miles from Windigo Pass where we'll turn left (west) and **continue on the #60 Road**. After turning west we arrive in one mile to the turnoff at Contorta Campground (see description below), located on the south shore of Crescent Lake. The #60 Road continues around Crescent Lake and to the town of Crescent Lake Junction.

HEADING NORTHWEST ON THE #700 ROAD:

After turning off the #60 Road, the #700 Road (Main Route) heads uphill towards its intersection with the #770 Road. After traveling uphill about two miles, keep an eye to the right for the #740 Road. This road is a little rutted but any car can navigate the short way to Linda Lake.

Linda Lake Campground: This tiny campsite (only one spot with a picnic table) is waterfront on Linda Lake, elevation 5,560 feet. The lake covers about four acres and is surrounded by tall trees. An outhouse (of sorts) is adjacent to the turnaround.

Trail #1494 to a pair of larger lakes starts at the campsite and heads uphill (north) to Lake Charline. After skirting shallow Lake Charline, the trail continues uphill and in about 1.5 miles arrives at 18-acre **Calamut Lake**, elevation 5,890 feet. There's a nice campground at the south end of Calamut with a view of Sawtooth Mountain, 1.5 miles to the north. Calamut is basically landlocked with no outlet; it's occasionally stocked with brook trout.

Back on the #700 Road we continue northwest for about three miles to our turn-off at the #770 Road.

#700 ROAD & #770 ROAD INTERSECTION:

Elevation 5,659 feet. **We turn right (north) on the #770 Road.**

This is a three-way intersection and the #700 Road continues west from here and back down to Lemolo Lake. This intersection is on the edge of a large forest fire that burned west of here in the recent past with many dead, standing trees evident in the distance.

Oregon Backroads Guide to the Pacific Crest Trail

The headwaters of the Willamette River, just below Lake Timpanogas.

Heading North on the #770 Road: On this road we cross the Calapooya Divide and enter the Middle Fork Willamette (pronounced will-LAM-mit) drainage. After leaving the #700 Road intersection, the #770 Road continues north and uphill to its crest at the intersection with the #2154 Road.

It's here that the waters divide and we leave the mighty Umpqua River drainage behind as we travel north. This pass has no official name so I nominate **"Calapooya Gap."**

The #770 Road officially ends here and becomes the #2154 Road as we continue north and head downhill on the #2154 Road. **The road to our left (west) is also confusingly labeled the #2154 Road but ignore the sign** (and this very rough road) **and stay on the main road heading downhill.**

The geographically significant **Calapooya Divide** is a roughly 60-mile-long ridge that runs east-west and divides the Umpqua River from the Willamette River. Named after the Native group that inhabited the area, the ridge begins in the west near I-5 and culminates in the east at 7,664-foot **Cowhorn Mountain** where the Umpqua, Willamette, and Deschutes Rivers divide.

Region 4 — Lemolo Lake to Odell Lake

Note the distinctive checkerboard pattern on the bark of this western white pine growing next to one of many small lakes in the area.

After leaving Calapooya Gap, the road heads downhill. In about a mile we come to the three-way intersection, (elevation 5,269 ft.) with the #362 Road to our left (west) and an **information sign** indicating **Summit Lake** and **Timpanogas Lake** to our right (east). From here we head east (turn right) on the #2154 Road.

Heading East on the #2154 Road: After leaving the **#362 Road intersection** we get glimpses of the Middle Willamette Valley to our left as we continue east on the #2154 Road towards Timpanogas Lake. In about 2.5 miles we encounter a beautiful mountain pond/lake next to the road, one of the many tarns dotting this part of the Central Oregon Cascades.

This is a great spot to turn off the road and look for bird life (herons) or let the dog go for a swim. The road begins to bend north and a half-mile past the pond, we come to the three-way intersection with the #270 Road heading north (downhill) and the #2154 Road turning east and uphill.

#2154 Road & #270 Road Intersection: Timpanogas Campground is just uphill and to the right on the #399 Road.

Oregon Backroads Guide to the Pacific Crest Trail

MAP R4.5: TIMPANOGAS LAKE TO WILLAMETTE PASS

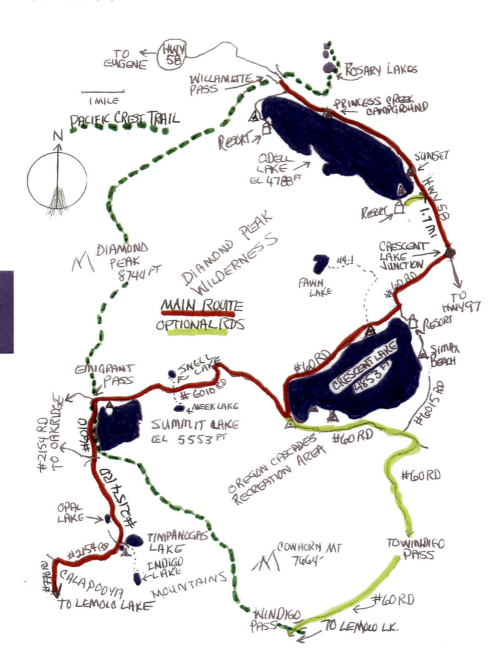

Region 4 — Lemolo Lake to Odell Lake

The #2154 Road heads north past Timpanogas Lake to the Opal Lake trailhead and on to Summit Lake.

Stop here and gaze down into the headwater of the most famous river in Oregon folklore. The waves of European American pioneers that made their way to the Oregon Country starting in the 1840s had heard stories of the fertile soils and mild climate of the **Willamette Valley**.

Most of the earliest emigrants braved the treacherous Columbia River to deliver them to the fabled land, and many lost their lives along the way. A toll road (the Barlow Road) was later developed to move wagons across the Cascades south of Mt. Hood, delivering travelers to the Sandy River and Oregon City. Beyond the money charged, the road certainly took its "toll" on man and beast as well; the country was rugged, the weather iffy, and the winding road crossed many raging streams.

Many travelers dreamed of a more direct way into the valley and a way was hacked out of the jungle covering the lower Middle Fork Willamette beginning in the early 1850s. The way was to be a "free" road with no toll and so the idea of the **Free Emigrant Road** was born. The first wagon train across the "road" encountered little more than blazed trees marking the way with huge logs of fallen trees crisscrossed like pickup sticks blocking their path. With beasts dying and people starving, the folks in the settlements around Eugene mounted a rescue. The survivors of the famous **"Lost Wagon Train"** nearly doubled the Euro American population of the Upper Willamette Valley in 1853.

Timpanogas Lake Campground: Timpanogas Lake draws solitude seekers and fishermen. There are 12 fee sites ($8) arrayed along the western shore of this 40-acre lake. There's a small boat launch at the entrance to the campground; no motors allowed on the lake. Right next door is lovely **Little Timpanogas**, which has no formal campsites. Both lakes hold brook trout.

There's a trailhead adjacent to the campground that connects with **Indigo Lake** and **June Lake**. It's about a mile and a half

Oregon Backroads Guide to the Pacific Crest Trail

Enjoy the quiet solitude of Lake Timpanogas, with just 12 campsites and no motorboats permitted.

with an elevation gain of over 700 feet to Indigo. A pleasant developed campsite at Indigo is located among the trees on the south shore. Sitting in a glacial, scooped basin, the south end of Indigo Lake abuts the steep, rocky north slope of **Sawtooth Mountain**. Sawtooth is part of the **Calapooya Mountains** and sits near the eastern end of that range. Cowhorn Mountain, two miles east of Sawtooth is the last of the Calapooya Mountains.

The trail continues past Indigo Lake and ascends to the ridgeline just east of Sawtooth Mountain and the junction of the Windy Pass Trail. Turn right at the junction and walk another short mile to the trail's highpoint. A side trail heads steeply up to the summit of Sawtooth Mountain. Look back the way you came and admire the pretty indigo waters of Indigo Lake below and Diamond Peak to the north. Look a mile and a half to the south and spy 18-acre Calamut Lake.

Opal Lake Trailhead: The trailhead is unmarked; look for a turnout on the left (west) side of the #2154 Road shortly after

Region 4 — Lemolo Lake to Odell Lake

leaving Lake Timpanogas. You can glimpse the pretty little lake through the towering trees as you start down the trail. The path heads down the old roadbed and quickly arrives at the lake shore. There is a small informal camp here and another camp (with a picnic table) located along the shore and among the big trees to the south.

Show up here in the early summer and you'll no doubt have the 10- to 12-acre lake to yourself (and a zillion skeeters). Late August and early September usually bring better weather and fewer winged bloodsuckers. It's close enough to the road to drag your inflatable boat or even wheel your kayak down the footpath for some floating fun. There's a scattering of (mostly small) brook trout in the lake; look for huckleberries along the shoreline and osprey in the trees.

Back on the #2154 Road: After leaving Opal Lake we continue north to the intersection with the #6010/Summit Lake Road. Along the way to the Summit Lake turn-off, the road continues uphill to its crest, a little more than a mile north from the Opal Lake Trail.

This high point is the actual **crest of the Cascades** where the road crosses over another unnamed pass. There's no sign here (as of 2013) but we cross over into eastern Oregon at this point and enter the **Deschutes National Forest** (and the Deschutes River drainage) and leave **Douglas County** as we enter **Klamath County**.

#2154 ROAD & #6010 ROAD INTERSECTION:
Elevation 5,663 ft.

We turn off the #2154 Road and head north on the #6010/ Summit Lake Road. The #2154 Road heads west from this 3-way intersection and arrives at Highway 58 near the town of Oakridge in about 40 miles.

The **#6010 Road** and the Main Route heads north and downhill and crosses the Pacific Crest Trail in 0.3 miles. An informal campsite here on Summit Lake is shared by hikers and car campers alike. With big views of Diamond Peak four miles to the north and an interesting looking island off shore, this is a pretty place indeed. The road doesn't touch the shore but it would be feasible to launch a kayak or canoe here.

Just over a mile from the crossing of the Pacific Crest Trail we arrive at **Summit Lake Campground** (no fee, 3 sites, and boat launch). The #6010 Road to the campground (1.4 miles) is negotiable by most any vehicle in good weather. Past the campground the #6010 Road becomes rocky and steep in places; **I don't recommend the road past the campground for any vehicle with low clearance.**

Summit Lake and Emigrant Pass: Amazingly beautiful Summit Lake, elevation 5,433 feet, is situated at the top of the Deschutes drainage and therefore has little inflow. Probably fed by springs, this more than 500-acre crystal clear lake maintains a pretty steady level throughout the summer months. The lake has many surprises for the paddler with hidden inlets and small islands scattered about. During the late spring and early summer melt-off, Summit Creek holds water and drains into Crescent Lake. The rest of the year the

Small islands dot Summit Lake. Diamond Peak dominates the horizon.

Region 4 — Lemolo Lake to Odell Lake

water sinks below the porous volcanic rocks and disappears along stretches of the creek and then reappears downstream.

Like Waldo Lake to the north, Summit Lake is incredibly clean and clear. With no silt and little algae to cloud the surface, visibility is almost unbelievable with the lake bottom clearly seen to depths exceeding 50 feet under calm conditions. Unfortunately for fishermen, these conditions do little to support aquatic animals like fish. The lake does support a small fishery and an occasional lake trout to 7 lbs. has been reportedly landed. Otherwise, mostly brook trout and kokanee are hooked here.

The **Pacific Crest Trail** parallels the western shore of Summit Lake as it makes its way towards **Emigrant Pass**. Located just above the small campground on the northwestern shore, 5,521 ft. Emigrant Pass is where the famous "Lost Wagon Train" of 1853 crossed the Cascade Crest headed for the Willamette Valley.

Later, the trail became the **Central Oregon Military Road**, upgraded in 1865 and 1866 to facilitate the movement of men and supplies during the Indian Wars of that era. The wagon road was reconstructed in the 1930s to accommodate modern vehicles. Deeply rutted, I don't recommend the Emigrant Pass road for anything but high-clearance, four-wheel-drive vehicles.

#6010 Road Heading East from Summit Lake:
⇨ **This road is not recommended for passenger cars.**

At the three-way intersection above the campground, there's a sign showing the way to Crescent Lake. It's a slow go on the #6010 Road past the Summit Lake Campground. Big rocks and steep hills present obstacles all the way to its end at Crescent Lake, just 6.2 miles from the campground. Large sections of this road are built on the old wagon road.

Look for a turn-out along the south side of the #6010 Road, 1.3 miles from the campground. A good-sized, unnamed lake lies a short way down the hill from here with a nice informal campsite along the shore.

Back on the road to Crescent Lake we soon encounter the trailhead marking the Meek Lake/Snell Lake Trailheads.

Meek Lake/Snell Lake Trailheads: Looking for some solitude? The country surrounding these four beautiful lakes offers that and more. Many more shallow ponds and small lakes can be found nearby that are attractive to both birds and animal life. All of this beautiful alpine environment also means gobs of breeding grounds for mosquitoes and many mosquitoes in the early season. Don't forget the DEET and the head-net.

Trailheads are on both sides of the road. The trail heading south crosses normally dry Summit Creek and winds through open woods before arriving at a bluff overlooking surprisingly deep **Meek Lake**. There's a small, informal campsite on the 10-acre lake with nothing more than a fire ring. It's about 0.4 miles to Meek Lake from the #6010 Road.

The trail heading north into the Diamond Peak Wilderness from the road goes to three lakes. **Farrell Lake**, on a short side-trail to the right off the main trail, is the first hikers will encounter. There's a campsite here and on Snell Lake. The trail turns west from Farrell Lake and soon arrives at **Snell Lake**. Tiny **Cornett Lake** lies to the north and east of Snell Lake. This is the southern edge of the Diamond Peak Wilderness with the

The boat launch at Crescent Lake Resort.

Region 4 — Lemolo Lake to Odell Lake

next road about 10 miles north as the crow flies. It's about 0.5 miles to Snell Lake from the road.

Back on the #6010 Road the way continues eastward and we arrive at the paved #60 Road and Crescent Lake in about 4 miles from the Meek Lake Trailhead.

CRESCENT LAKE AREA

Crescent Lake is 4,853 feet in elevation at the spillway and covers more than 5 square miles. This big, glacier-carved lake is over 250 feet deep. Although it's a natural lake, Crescent is used for irrigation. Consequently, lake levels are typically drawn down during the summer months.

Three Forest Service camps are at the lake, plus three group camps, a horse camp, four day-use areas, a comfortable resort, and a dog beach. If one of these doesn't work for you, many hiking and cycling opportunities are in the area too.

Some monster lake trout live in these waters and fishers with boats fight the persistent winds to troll the deep drop-offs and ledges where the big mackinaw live. Kokanee fishing can be very productive. Wind surfers, jet-skiers, and bigger sailboats love the wind and waves, and hot summer afternoons usually see them on the water.

The **Simax** area on the northeast side of the lake has two pumice beaches with sunny exposures and a group camp. The improved day-use areas both have vault toilets and cost $5. The north beach allows dogs, and the other doesn't. Two more day-use areas are on Crescent's southwestern shoreline — **Tandy Bay** and **Tranquil Cove**. Look for bald eagles in the late fall after the spawning fish.

Located at the northern end of the lake where Crescent Creek begins its journey east to the Little Deschutes River, **Crescent Lake Resort** has a café (try the fish tacos) and a full bar. While sitting next to the outdoor fireplace, you can sip a cold one on the pleasant patio overlooking the lake.

Crescent Lake Resort
541-433-2505

Oregon Backroads Guide to the Pacific Crest Trail

The dog beach at the Simax day-use area on Crescent Lake is cow-dog approved.

The resort has a small store and a fuel dock. The restaurant has a popular Sunday breakfast buffet, and the marina rents jet-skis, fishing boats, kayaks, paddle boards, and water bikes. The resort also rents mountain bikes, and during the winter, snowmobiles. They offer 18 cozy cabins for rent that are spread along the shore and among the trees. Dogs are welcome for an additional fee.

CAMPGROUNDS IN THE CRESCENT LAKE AREA

A variety of campgrounds to suit any style are available in the Crescent Lake area, including Contorta Point Campground, Spring Campground, Crescent Lake Campground, Windy Group Camp, Whitefish Horse Camp, and Simax Group Camp.

Contorta Point Campground & Group Camp: The name of this campground is derived from the scientific name for the lodge pole pine, *Pinus contorta*. This tree is ubiquitous to the highly fire-prone eastern slope of the Oregon Cascades and thick stands surround Crescent Lake.

Region 4 — Lemolo Lake to Odell Lake

The campground has 12 fee sites and a boat launch. The wide beach and pleasant day-use area draws the recreation crowd on summer weekends with watercraft of all descriptions lining the pumice shoreline. Water skiers, wake boarders, and jet-skiers dominate the water while sunbathers and stick-chasing dogs rule the beach.

The group camp section of Contorta Flats has 4 fee sites and can accommodate trailers to 40 feet.

Spring Campground: With 68 fee sites and a boat launch arrayed along the southern shore, this campground attracts plenty of campers on hot summer weekends. Many of the sites have waterfront access when the lake is full. Later in the season as the lake is drawn down for irrigation, a beach appears. The paved roads in the camp are ideal for families with bicycles, and the beach area is great for kids and dogs.

Crescent Lake Campground: Located on Simax Bay across from the resort, this campground has 46 fee sites and a boat launch. With the resort a stone's throw away, the campground

The volleyball net awaits campers at Contorta Point Campground.

Oregon Backroads Guide to the Pacific Crest Trail

One of the yurts for rent at Crescent Lake Campground.

has easy access to the store and restaurant too. Three yurts are available for rent, one of which is wheelchair accessible. Pets are not allowed in the yurts at this time. Call 1-877-444-6777 to reserve the yurts year-round.

The trail to **Fawn Lake** in the Diamond Peak Wilderness is adjacent to the campground. With an elevation gain of 800 feet, the trail to more than 40-acre Fawn Lake is about 2.5 miles long from the campground.

Windy Group Camp: It's down a pretty rough road to the campground. Nonetheless it's typical to find some massive 5th wheelers rounded up like a wagon train there. This camp has but one site and can accommodate trailers to 60 feet.

Whitefish Horse Camp: Located in the forest on the southwest corner of Crescent Lake, Whitefish Horse Camp has 19 sites, many with corrals. Most of the sites can accommodate trailers to 40 feet. **Whitefish Creek Trail #42** takes riders and hikers north from the camp to Diamond View Lake and the heart of the Diamond Peak Wilderness. The camp is on the opposite side of the road from the lake with no waterfront camps.

Region 4 — Lemolo Lake to Odell Lake

Simax Group Camp: Simax Group camp has 4 sites and can accommodate trailers to 30 feet. Located on the northeast side of Crescent Lake, the camp is close to the resort and the Simax Beach day-use area.

CRESCENT LAKE JUNCTION

The small town of Crescent Lake Junction lies two miles north of Crescent Lake along Highway 58 and serves as the commercial hub for Crescent and Odell Lakes. There's gas, groceries, a post office, and an extensive deli at the **Odell Sportsman Center**. The **Willamette Inn** provides motel accommodations in town. A little over a mile east on Highway 58, you'll find the **Crescent Creek Cottages** with kitchens, showers, and a laundry. There's room for RVs with full hook-ups from $30 a night.

Crescent Creek Cottages
541-433-2324

For a cold beer and decent food (broasted chicken is their specialty) try **Manley's Bar & Grill** in Crescent Lake Junction. Right next door to Manley's, try the Italian-themed **Casette di Pasta Restaurant** (with fantastic desserts).

Crescent Lake Junction even has a landing strip.

Views from the Odell Lodge marina on a clear spring morning.

Hwy. 58 Heading West: As we leave Crescent Lake Junction, notice the scorched trees that mark the recent wildfire that threatened the town in September 2008, stopped short by heroic effort. It's a little over one and a half miles to our turn-off to the left (south) to the East Access Road and Odell Lake Lodge.

ODELL LAKE AREA

Odell Lake is one of the largest natural lakes in the Oregon Cascades. More than five miles long and covering more than 3,500 acres, this glacier-carved lake is almost 300 feet deep at the east end near Odell Creek Campground. The lake is situated on the eastern side of Willamette Pass and surrounded by towering trees. At an elevation of 4,788 feet, the winds can be fierce, churning up whitecaps and blowing fishermen off the lake. Windsurfers, jet-skiers, and sailors of all descriptions take advantage of the reliable afternoon winds here.

More than thirty creeks and many springs keep the lake level at a near constant level throughout the summer and fall. Look for bald eagles at the creek mouths in the latter part of fall,

Region 4 — Lemolo Lake to Odell Lake

harvesting the fish spawning in the shallows. Trapper Creek is a good spot to look for eagles. The lake is served by four drive-in campgrounds and one boat-in camp. Two resorts are on the lake — Odell Lake Lodge on the east end and Shelter Cove Resort on the west end.

Fishing can be very good at Odell. Lake trout (also called mackinaw) were first stocked in 1902 and are now a self-sustaining population. The state record lake trout was taken from Odell in 1984, weighing in at 40 lbs, 8 ozs. Most macks caught in the lake average about 10 lbs. Some impressive rainbow trout to more than 20 inches are boated here annually.

There's also an abundant supply of kokanee (land-locked salmon) that are preyed upon by the big lake trout and bald eagles. First stocked in the lake in the early 1930s, their average length is about a foot with larger fish occasionally hooked. At this time fishermen are being encouraged to catch and keep up to 25 kokanee per day to reduce the population.

Odell Lake Lodge: So...how would you like to spend the night atop the terminal moraine of an extinct Cascade glacier? Here's your chance to do so in luxury. The mountain of ice that scooped out Odell Lake bulldozed the rocks and dirt that make up the southeast side of the lake where Odell Lake Lodge now resides.

If Diamond Lake Resort can be described as the "Mother of all Mountain Lake Resorts," Odell Lake Lodge would be the friendly Grandfather Resort. Founded in 1902, this is apparently the oldest of the mountain lake resorts in Oregon. Located on the east end of Odell Lake where Odell Creek begins, the dog-friendly resort offers cabins for rent year-round.

During the winter, this is ground zero for the cross-country ski crowd with many miles of trails at your doorstep. Skis, snow-shoes, and sleds are available for rent after the snow flies. The marina has moorage and offers boats for rent. The lodge has a restaurant (that serves excellent food) and an attractive patio overlooking the creek and the marina. On summer weekends, the lodge hosts live music on the patio next to the outdoor fireplace.

Oregon Backroads Guide to the Pacific Crest Trail

Morning mirrors itself at Princess Creek, Odell Lake.

The cabins are on the glacial ridge above the lake, many with magnificent views. For those seeking peace and quiet, request cabin #17, the one at the end of the resort road.

Odell Lake Lodge
541-433-2540

CAMPGROUNDS IN THE ODELL LAKE AREA

Three campgrounds are available on the lake: Odell Creek Campground, Sunset Cove Campground, and Princess Creek Campground.

Odell Creek: Located on the east end of the lake adjacent to Odell Lake Lodge, Odell Creek Campground has 30 fee sites with several waterfront. A few of the camp sites are located on two small peninsulas with water on virtually three sides. A boat launch and drinking water are available, and with the resort so close, a restaurant and store too!

Sunset Cove Campground: This camp is located on the south side of Hwy 58 amid the towering trees. There's a boat

Region 4 — Lemolo Lake to Odell Lake

launch at adjacent Chinquapin Point with a fish cleaning station. The day-use area is promoted as a place for the wind surfing crowd, separate from the boat launch. It's $5 to use the day-use area. Sunset has 24 fee sites and wheelchair accessible facilities.

Princess Creek Campground: Located on the north side of Odell Lake with big views to the south of Diamond Peak, Princess Creek has two docks adjacent to the boat launch. The campground has water, handicap accessible toilets, and 46 fee sites, some which can accommodate trailers to 50 feet.

The large day-use area is east of the boat landing with a sunny southern exposure. This is another beach where the wind is reliable in the afternoons and wind jockeys can show off their stuff.

Back on Highway 58 heading west we soon come to the West Lake Access Road (the road to Shelter Cove Resort), the Pacific Crest Trail, the Willamette Pass Ski Area, and the beginning of Volume Two — Willamette Pass to the Bridge of the Gods.

The jetty protecting Sunset Cove has a sidewalk to the end.

Oregon Backroads Guide to the Pacific Crest Trail

END OF REGION FOUR & VOLUME ONE

So here we are at Willamette Pass! Looking back at our journey, I feel nothing but happy for taking the trip so far…Taking the time to explore the high country of southwest Oregon has given me a sense of connection to this dramatic landscape in all its seasons. My imagination has taken me back thousands of years when the out-riders of our human family walked these trails, explored these mountain ridges, and fished these rivers.

The state we now call Oregon is in many ways arbitrary, a construction of European powers originally, and later on American invasion by (wagon train) settlers of the mid-nineteenth century. The dust seems to be settled for now with boundaries marked, and I'm thinking Oregon inherited a pretty fair share of beauty… in fact enough to fill up two books easily. I hope you'll join us in Volume Two as we explore northern Oregon from Willamette Pass to the Columbia River and the Bridge of the Gods

The cowdog (Brio) has woofed his consent to explore northern Oregon, and I whole heartedly agree.

South Sister beckons us to continue the journey into northern Oregon.

INDEX

A

American White Pelican 79, 95
Anderson Springs 120
Annie Creek 110
Annie Creek Rest Area 110
Annie Creek Restaurant 114
Annie Spring Entrance Station 103, 113
Applegate Lake 32, 34
Applegate Peak 117
Applegate River 10, 28, 31, 32, 34, 47
Applegate Trail 57, 70
Applegate Valley 19, 21, 22, 31, 34, 47
Ashland 7, 21, 22, 56, 57, 59, 61, 65, 68
Ashland Creek 67
Ashland Mountain House 56, 57
Ashland Ranger Station 21
Ashland Watershed 67
Aspen Inn Motel 107
Aspen Point Campground 87
avocet 95

B

bald eagle 174–175
Barlow Toll Road 163
Barron family 57
Beaver Creek Road 22, 30, 32–34
Bella Union Restaurant and Saloon 26
belted kingfisher 33

Benchmark Maps 14, 21, 104, 143
Birds Point Road 135, 139, 148
Big Draw Creek 83
Big Red Mountain 44–45
Big Spring 82
BLM 62, 74
Blue Ledge Mine 31
Boomtown Saloon 26
Bridge of the Gods 177, 178
Britt Music Festival (Britt Fest) 26
Britt, Peter 26–27
Britt Trails 28
Broken Arrow Campground 133
Brown Mountain 85
Buckhorn Road 70
Buckhorn Springs Retreat Center 70–71
Bunker Hill Campground 153

C

Calapooya Divide 140, 160
Calapooya Gap 160–161
Calapooya Mountains 143, 164
caldera 117
California Street 26
Callahan's Lodge 55
Calumet Lake 159, 164
Campers Cove Resort (Hyatt Lake Resort) 74–75, 77
Cantrell-Buckley Park 30
Cascade Mountains 7, 12, 61, 65, 70, 72, 122, 161

Cascade-Siskiyou National Monument 8, 62, 76
Cascade-Siskiyou National Monument Information Center 74
Casetta di Pasta Restaurant 173
Castle Rock 121
Central Oregon Military Road 167
chanterelle mushroom 83
Chiloquin 107
chinquapin tree 76
Chinquapin Point 176
Clearwater Falls 135
Cleetwood Cove Trailhead 124–125
Cloudcap Overlook 121
Colestin Valley 53
Columbia River 9, 163, 178
Contorta Point Campground 159, 170–171
Cornett Lake 168
Cow Creek Glade 35, 39, 40–44, 49
Cowhorn Mountain 160, 164
Crater Lake 27, 101, 111, 143, 173
Crater Lake Lodge 103, 112, 115
Crater Lake National Park 100, 103–104, 106–107, 110–112
Crescent Creek 169
Crescent Creek Cottages 173
Crescent Lake 157, 159, 166, 167, 169, 170
Crescent Lake Campground 170–172

Crescent Lake Junction 143, 157, 159, 173
Crescent Lake Resort 168–169
Crescent Ranger Station 143
Crystal Creek 93
Crystal Springs Campground 153–154
Crystal Springs Lodge 97–98
Crystal Springs Recreation Site 97

D

Dead Indian Memorial Road 68, 82–83, 85, 90
Deadman's Curve 34
Dellenback Trail 128
Deschutes National Forest 143, 165
Deschutes River 140, 160
Diamond Lake 100, 103–104, 126, 128–129
Diamond Lake Campground 132
Diamond Lake Corrals 132
Diamond Lake Ranger District 103, 104, 143
Diamond Lake Recreation Area 126
Diamond Lake Resort 126, 131–132
Diamond Lake RV Park 132
Diamond Peak 157, 164–166, 177
Diamond Peak Wilderness 168–169, 172
Donomore Creek 39
Donomore Meadow 22, 35, 37, 39

Index

Doppler Radar Station 51
Douglas County 165
Dread and Terror 151
Druids 49
Dutchman Peak 37
Dutchman Peak Lookout 22, 33, 35–37, 40, 43
Dutton Ridge 118

E

East Access Road 174
East Lemolo Lake Campground 139, 146, 153
East Rim Road 103, 113, 115, 123
Elliot Creek 34
Emigrant Creek 70
Emigrant Lake 10, 19, 21, 68
Emigrant Lake Park 57, 68
Emigrant Pass 166–167
Eugene 65

F

Farrell Lake 168
Fawn Lake 172
Forest Service Road #20 8–9, 21–22, 33–34, 36, 40, 47–51, 53
Forest Service Road #60 144, 155, 157–158, 169
Forest Service Road #3100 97, 99–100
Fort Klamath 58, 59, 61, 84, 100, 103, 106, 108
Fort Klamath, Historic 108
Free Emigrant Road 163
fulgarite 131

G

GPS 6
Grayback Road 113, 120
Great Meadow 89
Green Springs Inn 58, 68, 73–76
Green Springs Summit 70, 72–74
Griffin Pass 61, 82
Grouse Creek Glade 51
Grouse Gap 48, 50
Grouse Gap shelter 50

H

Harriman Creek 93
Highway 58 157, 165, 173–174, 177
Highway 62 106, 113
Highway 66 56–57, 61, 68, 70–74
Highway 99 (see Old Highway 99)
Highway 138 125–126, 133, 135
Highway 140 86, 88–91
Highway 230 126
Highway 238 24, 27–28
Hillman Peak 118
Hobart Bluff 71, 73
Hornbrook Formation 69
Howard Prairie Dam Road 76, 78, 80
Howard Prairie Lake 61
Howard Prairie Lake Recreation Area 78–79
Howard Prairie Lake Resort 78–80

Oregon Backroads Guide to the Pacific Crest Trail

Hyatt Lake 61, 74, 76–77, 79
Hyatt Lake Campground 74, 76
Hyatt Lake Resort (Campers Cove) 74–75, 77
Hyatt Prairie Road 74, 76–78

I

Iditarod 98
Indigo Lake 163–164
Inlet Campground 139, 153
Interstate 5 3, 48, 51, 54–55, 61

J

Jackson Creek 27
Jackson Gap 8, 36–37, 39, 40, 44
Jackson Park 32–33
Jacksonville 19–22
Jacksonville Barber Shop 26
Jacksonville Hill 28
Jo's Motel 100, 107–108
June Lake 163

K

Keene Creek 73, 75
Keene Creek Reservoir 74
Kelsay Horse Camp 151
Keno Access Road 80–82
Kerr Notch 118
Kimball State Park 109
Klamath Basin 95–96
Klamath Basin National Wildlife Refuge 96
Klamath Birding Trail 98
Klamath County 85
Klamath Falls 91
Klamath Lake 92

Klamath Mountains 7, 37
Klamath River 41, 47, 95
Klum Landing Campground 80
kokanee 153

L

Lake Charline 159
Lake Creek 129
Lake in Legend Overlook 123–124
Lake of the Woods 58, 84–86
Lake of the Woods Resort 85–88
Lake of the Woods Resort Road 86, 89
Lake Timpanogas 139, 160–161
lazuli bunting 46
Lemolo Falls 139, 149–150
Lemolo Lake 100–103, 133, 135, 140–143, 146, 153
Lemolo Lake Resort 104, 135, 139, 143, 148–149, 151
Linda Lake Campground 159
Lithia Park 59, 66–67
Little Applegate River 47
Little Deschutes River 169
Little Hyatt Lake 73–74
Little Timpanogas Lake 163
lodge pole pine 170
Long John Saddle 44, 46–48
Lost Creek Campground 113, 120
Lost Wagon Train 163, 167
Louie's Bar and Grill 65
Lovett, Lyle 19

M

Maidu Lake 151

★ *182* ★

Index

Malone Springs 96–97
Malone Springs Boat Launch 96–97
Malone Springs Campground 96
Manley's Bar and Grill 173
Maple Dell Road 34
Marley, Bob 2
Mazama Village Campground 113
McDonald Peak 50
McKee Covered Bridge 31–32
Medford 24, 126
Meek Lake 167–168
Meridian Overlook 48–50
Middle Fork Willamette River 160–161, 163
Modoc Indian Wars 108–109
mountain bluebird 46
Mountain Lakes Wilderness 86
Mt. Ashland 33, 36, 42, 46, 48, 50–51, 53
Mt. Ashland Campground 51–52
Mt. Ashland Road 54
Mt. Ashland Ski Area 52, 54
Mt. Ashland Summit Road 51
Mt. Bailey 126, 128–129
Mt. Bailey Trail 130
Mt. Everest 6
Mt. Hood 5, 163
Mt. Mazama 101, 117, 122–123, 128–129
Mt. McLoughlin 47–48, 62, 85–86, 118
Mt. Scott 59, 118, 123

Mt. Scott Trail 121–123
Mt. Shasta 9, 37, 41, 50, 118
Mt. Thielsen 117–118, 128, 130, 146
Mt. Thielsen Trail 131
Mt. Thielsen Viewpoint 126
Mt. Thielsen Wilderness 151

N

Nicholson Road 10
North Entrance Station 103, 113, 126
North Junction 125
North Umpqua River 100, 137, 150, 154–155, 158
North Umpqua Trail 149, 151

O

Oakridge 165
Oakridge Ranger Station 143
Observation Peak 35, 40–43
Observation Peak Botanical Area (See Cow Creek Glade)
Odell Creek 175–176
Odell Creek Campground 174
Odell Lake 141, 174, 177
Odell Lake Lodge 174–176
Odell Sportsman Center 173
Odessa 91–92
Odessa Creek Campground 91
Oldenburg Lake Trail 158
Old Highway 99 22, 56, 70
Opal Lake Trail 163–164
Oregon City 163
Oregon Shakespeare Festival 67
osprey 77, 139
Osprey Viewing Area 78

P

Pacific Crest Trail 3–10, 21, 35–39, 43–44, 46–50, 53, 55–56, 67, 73–74, 76, 82, 85–86, 111–113, 130, 159, 165–167, 177
Pacific Corp 137, 146
paintbrush, common 154
paintbrush, Indian 154
Pederson Snow Park 79, 85
Pelican Butte 90, 118
Phantom Ship 116, 118
Phantom Ship Overlook 118–119
Pilot Rock 71–72
Pinnacles Road 115–116, 118
Pinnacles Overlook 118–119
Pit Lakes Trail 139
Plaikni Falls 119–120
Point Comfort Lodge 92
Poole Creek Campground 139, 146, 153
Princess Creek Campground 176–177
Pumice Desert 125–126
Pumice Castle Overlook 121

R

Rainbow Bay Picnic Area 87
Red Buttes 34
Red Buttes Wilderness 34
Red Cone 125
Rocky Point 62, 91–92
Rocky Point Boat Launch 93, 97
Rocky Point Resort 93–94
Rocky Point Road 88–92

Rogue River 41, 47
Rogue River National Forest 61, 104
Ruch 22, 27–30

S

Sand Creek 120
sand hill crane 79, 95
Sandy River 163
Santiam Pass 83
Sawtooth Mountain 159, 165
serpentine 41
Seven Mile Creek 44
Seven Mile Road 175, 177
Sheep Camp Springs Road 44
Shelter Cove Resort 175, 177
Silver Fork Gap 22, 33–40, 43
Simax Bay 171
Simax Beach Day-Use Area 169–170, 173
Simax Group Camp 170, 173
Siskiyou Crest Road 21
Siskiyou Gap 45–46
Siskiyou Mountains 7, 12, 21, 43, 48–50, 53–54, 65, 72
Siskiyou Peak/Trail 49–50
Siskiyou Ranger District 61, 103
Siskiyou Summit 51
Sky Lakes Wilderness 86
Snell Lake 167–169
Soda Mountain Road 73
Soda Mountain Wilderness 8, 62, 70, 72, 74, 76
South Shore Day-Use Area 133
South Shore Pizza Parlor 128
Southern Oregon University 66

Index

South Stage Cellars 25
Spring Campground 157, 170–171
Spring River 153–155
Standing Stone Brewery 66
Star Thistle 28
Star Ranger Station 21, 30
Steel Visitors' Center 113–114
stonecrop 146
Summit Creek 166–168
Summit Lake 143, 161, 163, 165–167
Summit Lake Campground 166–167
sugar pine 83
Sun Notch 116
Sun Pass Ranch 107
Sunset Campground 87
Sunset Cove Boat Launch 176
Sunset Cove Campground 176–177

T

Talent 48
Tandy Bay Day-Use Area 169
Thielsen Creek Forest Camp 135
Thielsen View Campground 133
Timpanogas Lake 163
Timpanogas Campground 161, 163
Tokatee Falls 137
Tranquil Cove Day-Use Area 169
Trapper Creek 175
trillium 149
Trinity Alps 50
Tyler Creek Road 70–71

U

Umpqua Hot Springs 151
Umpqua River 160
Umpqua National Forest 103–104, 132, 143
Union Peak 118
Upper Applegate River Road 27–28, 30–32
Upper Klamath Basin 59, 94, 106, 108, 118
Upper Klamath Lake 11, 58, 61, 91, 93 95–96
Upper Klamath Lake Canoe Trail 11, 93, 96–97
Upper Klamath Lake National Wildlife Refuge 95–96

V

Valley View Winery 30
Vidae Falls 114–116
Vidae Ridge 117

W

Wagner Creek 48
Warm Springs Creek Falls Trail 149, 151–153
Washington State 9
Water Ouzel 33
Watchman Peak 118
Watson Falls 136–137
western white pine 161
West Rim Road 103, 113
Westside Road 89–91, 99
Whitefish Creek Trail 172
Whitefish Horse Camp 170, 172
White Mule Trail 151

★ 185 ★

Whitehorse Falls 136
whitebark pine 122
Whitebark Pine Picnic Area 122–123
Wildcat Campground 77
Willamette Inn 173
Willamette Meridian 49
Willamette Pass 140–143, 174, 177–178
Willamette Pass Ski Area 177
Willamette River 140, 160
Willamette River Valley 163
Willow Point Campground 80
Windigo Pass 143, 155, 157–159
Windigo Pass Road 139– 155–157
Windy Group Camp 170
Windy Pass Trail 164
Winema National Forest 62, 85, 110
Wizard Island 112. 118, 125
Woodrat Mountain 28
Wood River 106, 108–110
Wood River Day-Use Area 109
Wood River, head of the 109–110
World of Wine Festival 25
Wrangle Campground 45
Wrangle Gap 44–46, 48

Y
yurts 172